The Giver

LOIS LOWRY

Long tail Books

THE GIVER

ISBN 979-11-91343-86-1 14740

Longtail Books

For all the children

To whom we entrust the future

1

It was almost December, and Jonas was beginning to be **frighten**ed. No. Wrong word, Jonas thought. Frightened meant that deep, **sicken**ing feeling of something terrible about to happen. Frightened was the way he had felt a year ago when an **unidentified aircraft** had **overflown** the community twice. He had seen it both times. **Squint**ing toward the sky, he had seen the **sleek** jet, almost a **blur** at its high speed, go past, and a second later heard the **blast** of sound that followed. Then one more time, a moment later, from the opposite direction, the same plane.

At first, he had been only **fascinated**. He had never seen aircraft so close, for it was against the rules for Pilots to fly over the community. **Occasional**ly, when supplies were delivered by **cargo** planes to the landing field across the river, the children rode their bicycles to the **riverbank** and watched, **intrigued**, the **unload**ing and then the takeoff directed to the west, always away from the community.

But the aircraft a year ago had been different. It was not a **squat, fat-bellied** cargo plane but a **needle-nosed** single-pilot jet. Jonas, looking around **anxious**ly, had seen others—adults as well as children—stop what they were doing and wait, confused, for an explanation of the frightening event.

Then all of the citizens had been ordered to go into the nearest building and stay there. IMMEDIATELY, the **rasp**ing voice through the speakers had said. LEAVE YOUR BICYCLES WHERE THEY ARE.

Instantly, **obedient**ly, Jonas had dropped his bike on its side on the path behind his family's **dwelling**. He had run indoors and stayed there, alone. His parents were both at work, and his little sister, Lily, was at the Childcare Center where she spent her after-school hours. Looking through the front window, he had seen no people: none of the busy afternoon crew of Street Cleaners, Landscape Workers, and Food Delivery people who usually **populate**d the community at that time of day. He saw only the **abandon**ed bikes here and there on their sides; an **upturned** wheel on one was still **revolving** slowly.

He had been frightened then. The sense of his own community silent, waiting, had made his stomach **churn**. He had **trembled**.

But it had been nothing. Within minutes the speakers had **crackled** again, and the voice, **reassuring** now and less **urgent**, had explained that a Pilot-in-Training had **misread** his **navigational** instructions and made a wrong turn. **Desperate**ly the Pilot had been trying to make his way back before his error was noticed.

NEEDLESS TO SAY, HE WILL BE RELEASED, the voice had said, followed by silence. There was an ironic tone to that final message, as if the Speaker found it **amusing**; and Jonas had smiled a little, though he knew what a **grim** statement it had been. For a **contributing** citizen to be released from the community was a final decision, a terrible **punish**ment, an **overwhelm**ing statement of failure.

Even the children were **scold**ed if they used the term lightly at play, **jeer**ing at a teammate who missed a catch or **stumble**d in a race. Jonas had done it once, had shouted at his best friend, "That's it, Asher! You're released!" when Asher's **clumsy** error had lost a match for his team. He had been taken aside for a brief and serious talk by the coach, had **hung his head** with **guilt** and **embarrass**ment, and **apologize**d to Asher after the game.

Now, thinking about the feeling of fear as he **pedal**ed home along the river path, he remembered that moment of **palpable**, stomach-**sink**ing terror when the aircraft had **streak**ed above. It was not what he was feeling now with

December approaching. He searched for the right word to describe his own feeling.

Jonas was careful about language. Not like his friend, Asher, who talked too fast and mixed things up, **scrambling** words and **phrase**s until they were **barely recognizable** and often very funny.

Jonas **grin**ned, remembering the morning that Asher had **dash**ed into the classroom, late as usual, arriving **breathless**ly in the middle of the **chant**ing of the morning **anthem**. When the class took their seats at the conclusion of the **patriotic hymn**, Asher remained standing to make his public **apology** as was required.

"I apologize for **inconveniencing** my learning community." Asher ran through the standard apology phrase rapidly, still catching his breath. The Instructor and class waited **patient**ly for his explanation. The students had all been grinning, because they had listened to Asher's explanations so many times before.

"I left home at the correct time but when I was riding along near the **hatchery**, the crew was separating some **salmon**. I guess I just got **distraught**, watching them.

"I apologize to my classmates," Asher concluded. He **smooth**ed his **rumpled tunic** and sat down.

"We accept your apology, Asher." The class **recite**d the standard response **in unison**. Many of the students were biting their lips to keep from laughing.

"I accept your apology, Asher," the Instructor said. He was smiling. "And I thank you, because once again you have provided an opportunity for a lesson in language. 'Distraught' is too strong an adjective to describe salmon-viewing." He turned and wrote "distraught" on the instructional board. Beside it he wrote "**distract**ed."

Jonas, nearing his home now, smiled at the **recollection**. Thinking, still, as he wheeled his bike into its narrow **port** beside the door, he realized that frightened was the wrong word to describe his feelings, now that December was almost here. It was too strong an adjective.

He had waited a long time for this special December. Now that it was almost upon him, he wasn't frightened, but he was . . . **eager**, he decided. He was eager for it to come. And he was excited, certainly. All of the Elevens were excited about the event that would be coming so soon.

But there was a little **shudder** of nervousness when he thought about it, about what might happen.

Apprehensive, Jonas decided. That's what I am.

"Who wants to be the first tonight, for feelings?" Jonas's father asked, at the conclusion of their evening meal.

It was one of the **ritual**s, the evening telling of feelings. Sometimes Jonas and his sister, Lily, argued over turns, over who would get to go first. Their parents, of course, were part of the ritual; they, too, told their feelings each evening. But like all parents—all adults—they didn't fight and **wheedle** for their turn.

Nor did Jonas, tonight. His feelings were too **complicated** this evening. He wanted to share them, but he wasn't eager to begin the process of **sifting through** his own complicated emotions, even with the help that he knew his parents could give.

"You go, Lily," he said, seeing his sister, who was much younger—only a Seven—**wiggling** with **impatience** in her chair.

"I felt very angry this afternoon," Lily announced. "My Childcare group was at the play area, and we had a visiting group of Sevens, and they didn't **obey** the rules at *all*. One of them—a male; I don't know his name—kept going right to the front of the line for the slide, even though the rest of us were all waiting. I felt so angry at him. I made my hand into a **fist**, like this." She held up a **clench**ed fist and the rest of the family smiled at her small **defiant** gesture.

"Why do you think the visitors didn't obey the rules?" Mother asked.

Lily considered, and shook her head. "I don't know. They acted like . . . like . . . "

"Animals?" Jonas suggested. He laughed.

"That's right," Lily said, laughing too. "Like animals." Neither child knew what the word meant, exactly, but it was often used to describe someone uneducated or clumsy, someone who didn't fit in.

"Where were the visitors from?" Father asked. Lily **frowned**, trying to remember. "Our leader told us, when he made the welcome speech, but I can't remember. I guess I wasn't paying attention. It was from another community. They had to leave very early, and they had their midday meal on the bus."

Mother nodded. "Do you think it's possible that their rules may be different? And so they simply didn't know what your play area rules were?"

Lily **shrugged**, and nodded. "I suppose."

"You've visited other communities, haven't you?" Jonas asked. "My group has, often."

Lily nodded again. "When we were Sixes, we went and shared a whole school day with a group of Sixes in their community."

"How did you feel when you were there?"

Lily frowned. "I felt strange. Because their methods were different. They were learning **usages** that my group hadn't learned yet, so we felt stupid."

Father was listening with interest. "I'm thinking, Lily," he said, "about the boy who didn't obey the rules today. Do you think it's possible that he felt strange and stupid, being in a new place with rules that he didn't know about?"

Lily **pondered** that. "Yes," she said, finally.

"I feel a little sorry for him," Jonas said, "even though I don't even know him. I feel sorry for anyone who is in a place where he feels strange and stupid."

"How do you feel now, Lily?" Father asked. "Still angry?"

"I guess not," Lily decided. "I guess I feel a little sorry for him. And sorry I made a fist." She grinned.

Jonas smiled back at his sister. Lily's feelings were always **straightforward**, fairly simple, usually easy to **resolve**. He guessed that his own had been, too, when he was a Seven.

He listened politely, though not very **attentively**, while his father took his turn, describing a feeling of worry that he'd had that day at work: a concern about one of the newchildren who wasn't doing well. Jonas's father's title was **Nurturer**. He and the other Nurturers were responsible for all the physical and emotional needs of every newchild during its earliest life. It was a very important job, Jonas knew, but it wasn't one that interested him much.

"What **gender** is it?" Lily asked.

"Male," Father said. "He's a sweet little male with a lovely **disposition**. But he isn't growing as fast as he should, and he doesn't **sleep soundly**. We have him in the extra care section for **supplementary** nurturing, but the **committee**'s beginning to talk about releasing him."

"Oh, *no*," Mother **murmur**ed **sympathetic**ally. "I know how sad that must make you feel."

Jonas and Lily both nodded sympathetically as well. Release of newchildren was always sad, because they hadn't had a chance to enjoy life within the community yet. And they hadn't done anything wrong.

There were only two **occasion**s of release which were not punishment. Release of the **elder**ly, which was a time of **cele-bration** for a life well and fully lived; and release of a new-child, which always brought a sense of what-could-we-have-done. This was especially troubling for the Nurturers, like Father, who felt they had failed somehow. But it happened very **rare**ly.

"Well," Father said, "I'm going to keep trying. I may ask the committee for **permission** to bring him here at night, if you don't mind. You know what the night-crew Nurturers are like. I think this little guy needs something extra."

"Of course," Mother said, and Jonas and Lily nodded. They had heard Father complain about the night crew before. It was a lesser job, night-crew nurturing, **assign**ed to those who lacked the interest or skills or **insight** for the more **vital** jobs of the daytime hours. Most of the people on the night crew had not even been given **spouse**s because they lacked, somehow, the essential **capacity** to connect to others, which was required for the creation of a family unit.

"Maybe we could even keep him," Lily suggested sweetly, trying to look **innocent**. The look was fake, Jonas knew; they all knew.

"Lily," Mother reminded her, smiling, "you know the rules."

Two children—one male, one female—to each family unit. It was written very clearly in the rules.

Lily **giggle**d. "Well," she said, "I thought maybe just this once."

Next, Mother, who held a **prominent** position at the Department of **Justice**, talked about her feelings. Today a repeat **offender** had been brought before her, someone who had broken the rules before. Someone who she hoped had been **adequate**ly and fairly punished, and who had been **restore**d to his place: to his job, his home, his family unit. To see him brought before her a second time caused her overwhelming feelings of **frustration** and anger. And even guilt, that she hadn't made a difference in his life.

"I feel frightened, too, for him," she **confess**ed. "You know that there's no third chance. The rules say that if there's a third **transgression**, he simply has to be released."

Jonas **shivered**. He knew it happened. There was even a boy in his group of Elevens whose father had been released years before. No one ever mentioned it; the **disgrace** was **unspeakable**. It was hard to imagine.

Lily stood up and went to her mother. She **stroke**d her mother's arm.

From his place at the table, Father reached over and took her hand. Jonas reached for the other.

One by one, they comforted her. Soon she smiled, thanked them, and murmured that she felt **soothe**d.

The ritual continued. "Jonas?" Father asked. "You're last, tonight."

Jonas sighed. This evening he almost would have preferred to keep his feelings hidden. But it was, of course, against the rules.

"I'm feeling apprehensive," he confessed, glad that the **appropriate descriptive** word had finally come to him.

"Why is that, son?" His father looked concerned.

"I know there's really nothing to worry about," Jonas explained, "and that every adult has been through it. I know you have, Father, and you too, Mother. But it's the **Ceremony** that I'm apprehensive about. It's almost December."

Lily looked up, her eyes wide. "The Ceremony of Twelve," she whispered in an **awe**d voice. Even the smallest children—Lily's age and younger—knew that it **lay** in the future for each of them.

"I'm glad you told us of your feelings," Father said.

"Lily," Mother said, **beckon**ing to the little girl, "Go on now and get into your nightclothes. Father and I are going to stay here and talk to Jonas for a while."

Lily sighed, but obediently she got down from her chair. "Privately?" she asked.

Mother nodded. "Yes," she said, "this talk will be a private one with Jonas."

2

Jonas watched as his father **pour**ed a fresh cup of coffee. He waited.

"You know," his father finally said, "every December was exciting to me when I was young. And it has been for you and Lily, too, I'm sure. Each December brings such changes."

Jonas nodded. He could remember the Decembers back to when he had become, well, probably a Four. The earlier ones were lost to him. But he **observe**d them each year, and he remembered Lily's earliest Decembers. He remembered when his family received Lily, the day she was named, the day that she had become a One.

The **Ceremony** for the Ones was always noisy and fun. Each December, all the newchildren born in the previous year turned One. One at a time—there were always fifty in each year's group, if none had been **released**—they had been brought to the stage by the **Nurturer**s who had cared for them since birth. Some were already walking, **wobbly** on their **unsteady** legs; others were no more than a few days old, wrapped in **blanket**s, held by their Nurturers.

"I enjoy the Naming," Jonas said.

His mother agreed, smiling. "The year we got Lily, we knew, of course, that we'd receive our female, because we'd made our **application** and been **approve**d. But I'd been wondering and wondering what her name would be.

"I could have **sneak**ed a look at the list prior to the ceremony," Father **confide**d. "The **committee** always makes the list in advance, and it's right there in the office at the Nurturing Center.

"**As a matter of fact**," he went on, "I feel a little **guilty** about this. But I *did* go in this afternoon and looked to see if this year's Naming list had been made yet. It was right there in the office, and I looked up number Thirty-six—that's the little guy I've been concerned about—because it occurred to me that it might **enhance** his nurturing if I could call him by a name. Just privately, of course, when no one else is around."

"Did you find it?" Jonas asked. He was **fascinate**d. It didn't seem a terribly important rule, but the fact that his father had broken a rule at all **awe**d him. He **glance**d at his mother, the one responsible for **adherence** to the rules, and was **relieve**d that she was smiling.

His father nodded. "His name—if he makes it to the Naming without being released, of course—is to be Gabriel. So I whisper that to him when I feed him every four hours, and during exercise and playtime. If no one can hear me.

"I call him Gabe, actually," he said, and **grin**ned.

"Gabe." Jonas tried it out. A good name, he decided.

Though Jonas had only become a Five the year that they **acquire**d Lily and learned her name, he remembered the excitement, the conversations at home, wondering about her: how she would look, who she would be, how she would fit into their **establish**ed family unit. He remembered climbing the steps to the stage with his parents, his father by his side that year instead of with the Nurturers, since it was the year that he would be given a newchild of his own.

He remembered his mother taking the newchild, his sister, into her arms, while the document was read to the **assemble**d family units. "Newchild Twenty-three," the Namer had read. "Lily."

He remembered his father's look of delight, and that his father had whispered, "She's one of my favorites. I was hoping for her to be the one." The crowd had **clap**ped, and Jonas had grinned. He liked his sister's name. Lily, **barely** awake, had waved her small **fist**. Then they had stepped down to make room for the next family unit.

"When I was an Eleven," his father said now, "as you are, Jonas, I was very **impatient**, waiting for the Ceremony of Twelve. It's a long two days. I remember that I enjoyed the Ones, as I always do, but that I didn't pay much attention to the other ceremonies, except for my sister's. She became a Nine that year, and got her bicycle. I'd been teaching her to ride mine, even though **technically** I wasn't supposed to."

Jonas laughed. It was one of the few rules that was not taken very seriously and was almost *always* broken. The children all received their bicycles at Nine; they were not allowed to ride bicycles before then. But almost always, the older brothers and sisters had secretly taught the younger ones. Jonas had been thinking already about teaching Lily.

There was talk about changing the rule and giving the bicycles at an earlier age. A committee was studying the idea. When something went to a committee for study, the people always joked about it. They said that the committee members would become **Elder**s by the time the rule change was made.

Rules were very hard to change. Sometimes, if it was a very important rule—unlike the one **govern**ing the age for bicycles—it would have to go, **eventually**, to The Receiver for a decision. The Receiver was the most important Elder. Jonas had never even seen him, that he knew of; someone in a position of such importance lived and worked alone. But the committee would never bother The Receiver with a question about bicycles; they would simply **fret** and argue about it themselves for years, until the citizens forgot that it had ever gone to them for study.

His father continued. "So I watched and cheered when my sister, Katya, became a Nine and removed her hair ribbons and got her bicycle," Father went on. "Then I didn't pay much attention to the Tens and Elevens. And *finally*, at the end of the second day, which seemed to go on forever, it was my turn. It was the Ceremony of Twelve."

Jonas **shiver**ed. He pictured his father, who must have been a shy and quiet boy, for he was a shy and quiet man, seated with his group, waiting to be called to the stage. The Ceremony of Twelve was the last of the Ceremonies. The most important.

"I remember how proud my parents looked—and my sister, too; even though she wanted to be out riding the bicycle publicly, she stopped **fidget**ing and was very still and **attentive** when my turn came.

"But to be honest, Jonas," his father said, "for me there was not the **element** of **suspense** that there is with your Ceremony. Because I was already fairly certain of what my

Assignment was to be."

Jonas was surprised. There was no way, really, to know in advance. It was a secret selection, made by the leaders of the community, the Committee of Elders, who took the responsibility so seriously that there were never even any jokes made about Assignments.

His mother seemed surprised, too. "How could you have known?" she asked.

His father smiled his gentle smile. "Well, it was clear to me—and my parents later **confessed** that it had been obvious to them, too—what my **aptitude** was. I had always loved the newchildren more than anything. When my friends in my age group were holding bicycle races, or building toy **vehicle**s or bridges with their **construction** sets, or—"

"All the things I do with my friends," Jonas pointed out, and his mother nodded in agreement.

"I always participated, of course, because as children we must experience all of those things. And I studied hard in school, as you do, Jonas. But again and again, during free time, I found myself drawn to the newchildren. I spent almost all of my **volunteer** hours helping in the Nurturing Center. Of course the Elders knew that, from their **observation**."

Jonas nodded. During the past year he had been aware

of the increasing level of observation. In school, at recreation time, and during volunteer hours, he had noticed the Elders watching him and the other Elevens. He had seen them taking notes. He knew, too, that the Elders were meeting for long hours with all of the instructors that he and the other Elevens had had during their years of school.

"So I expected it, and I was pleased, but not at all surprised, when my Assignment was announced as Nurturer," Father explained.

"Did everyone **applaud**, even though they weren't surprised?" Jonas asked.

"Oh, of course. They were happy for me, that my Assignment was what I wanted most. I felt very fortunate." His father smiled.

"Were any of the Elevens disappointed, your year?" Jonas asked. Unlike his father, he had no idea what his Assignment would be. But he knew that some would disappoint him. Though he respected his father's work, Nurturer would not be his wish. And he didn't **envy** Laborers at all.

His father thought. "No, I don't think so. Of course the Elders are so careful in their observations and selections."

"I think it's probably the most important job in our community," his mother commented.

"My friend Yoshiko was surprised by her selection as

Doctor," Father said, "but she was **thrill**ed. And let's see, there was Andrei—I remember that when we were boys he never wanted to do physical things. He spent all the recreation time he could with his construction set, and his volunteer hours were always on building sites. The Elders knew that, of course. Andrei was given the Assignment of Engineer and he was delighted."

"Andrei later designed the bridge that crosses the river to the west of town," Jonas's mother said. "It wasn't there when we were children."

"There are very **rare**ly disappointments, Jonas. I don't think you need to worry about that," his father **reassure**d him. "And if there are, you know there's an **appeal** process." But they all laughed at that—an appeal went to a committee for study.

"I worry a little about Asher's Assignment," Jonas confessed. "Asher's such *fun*. But he doesn't really have any serious interests. He makes a game out of everything."

His father **chuckle**d. "You know," he said, "I remember when Asher was a newchild at the Nurturing Center, before he was named. He never cried. He **giggle**d and laughed at everything. All of us on the staff enjoyed nurturing Asher."

"The Elders know Asher," his mother said. "They'll find exactly the right Assignment for him. I don't think you need to worry about him. But, Jonas, let me warn you about something that may not have occurred to you. I know I didn't think about it until after my Ceremony of Twelve."

"What's that?"

"Well, it's the last of the Ceremonies, as you know. After Twelve, age isn't important. Most of us even **lose track of** how old we are as time passes, though the information is in the Hall of Open Records, and we could go and look it up if we wanted to. What's important is the preparation for adult life, and the training you'll receive in your Assignment."

"I know that," Jonas said. "Everyone knows that."

"But it means," his mother went on, "that you'll move into a new group. And each of your friends will. You'll no longer be spending your time with your group of Elevens. After the Ceremony of Twelve, you'll be with your Assignment group, with those in training. No more volunteer hours. No more recreation hours. So your friends will no longer be as close."

Jonas shook his head. "Asher and I will always be friends," he said firmly. "And there will still be school."

"That's true," his father agreed. "But what your mother said is true as well. There will be changes."

"*Good* changes, though," his mother pointed out. "After

my Ceremony of Twelve, I missed my childhood recreation. But when I entered my training for Law and **Justice**, I found myself with people who shared my interests. I made friends on a new level, friends of all ages."

"Did you still play at all, after Twelve?" Jonas asked.

"**Occasionally**," his mother replied. "But it didn't seem as important to me."

"I did," his father said, laughing. "I still do. Every day, at the Nurturing Center, I play bounce-on-the-knee,* and peek-a-boo,■ and hug-the-teddy.★" He reached over and **stroked** Jonas's **neatly trimmed** hair. "Fun doesn't end when you become Twelve."

Lily appeared, wearing her nightclothes, in the doorway. She gave an impatient sigh. "This is certainly a very *long* private conversation," she said. "And there are certain people waiting for their comfort object.◆"

"Lily," her mother said **fondly**, "you're very close to being an Eight, and when you're an Eight, your comfort object will be taken away. It will be recycled to the younger children. You should be starting to go off to sleep without

---

* bounce-on-the-knee : 무릎을 굽혀 땅에 대고 콩콩 뛰는 놀이.

■ peek-a-boo : 얼굴을 가리거나 숨어 있다가 어린이를 놀리는 까꿍 놀이.

★ hug-the-teddy : 곰 인형을 안고 노는 것.

◆ comfort object : 아이들이 잠자리에서 껴안고 자는 담요나 봉제 인형 같이 정서적인 안정감(comfort)을 주는 물건(object).

it."

But her father had already gone to the **shelf** and taken down the **stuffed** elephant which was kept there. Many of the comfort objects, like Lily's, were soft, stuffed, **imaginary** creatures. Jonas's had been called a bear.

"Here you are, Lily-billy," he said. "I'll come help you remove your hair ribbons."

Jonas and his mother rolled their eyes, yet they watched **affectionate**ly as Lily and her father headed to her sleeping-room with the stuffed elephant that had been given to her as her comfort object when she was born. His mother moved to her big desk and opened her **briefcase**; her work never seemed to end, even when she was at home in the evening. Jonas went to his own desk and began to sort through his school papers for the evening's assignment. But his mind was still on December and the coming Ceremony.

Though he had been reassured by the talk with his parents, he hadn't the slightest idea what Assignment the Elders would be selecting for his future, or how he might feel about it when the day came.

3

"Oh, look!" Lily **squeal**ed in delight. "Isn't he cute? Look how tiny he is! And he has funny eyes like yours, Jonas!" Jonas **glare**d at her. He didn't like it that she had mentioned his eyes. He waited for his father to **chastise** Lily. But Father was busy un**strap**ping the carrying basket from the back of his bicycle. Jonas walked over to look.

It was the first thing Jonas noticed as he looked at the newchild **peer**ing up curiously from the basket. The pale eyes.

Almost every citizen in the community had dark eyes. His parents did, and Lily did, and so did all of his group members and friends. But there were a few **exception**s: Jonas himself, and a female Five who he had noticed had the different, lighter eyes. No one mentioned such things; it was not a rule, but was considered rude to call attention to things that were **unsettling** or different about **individuals**. Lily, he decided, would have to learn that soon, or she would be called in for chastisement because of her **insensitive chatter**.

Father put his bike into its **port**. Then he picked up the basket and carried it into the house. Lily followed behind, but she **glance**d back over her shoulder at Jonas and **tease**d, "Maybe he had the same Birthmother as you."

Jonas **shrugged**. He followed them inside. But he had been **startle**d by the newchild's eyes. Mirrors were rare in the community; they weren't **forbidden**, but there was no real need of them, and Jonas had simply never bothered to look at himself very often even when he found himself in a location where a mirror existed. Now, seeing the newchild and its expression, he was reminded that the light eyes were not only a **rarity** but gave the one who had them a certain look—what was it? ***Depth***, he decided; as if one were looking into the clear water of the river, down to the bottom, where things might **lurk** which hadn't been discovered yet. He felt **self-conscious**, realizing that he, too, had that look.

He went to his desk, pretending not to be interested in the newchild. On the other side of the room, Mother and Lily were bending over to watch as Father unwrapped its **blanket**.

"What's his comfort object called?" Lily asked, picking

up the **stuffed** creature which had been placed beside the newchild in his basket.

Father glanced at it. "**Hippo**," he said.

Lily giggled at the strange word. "Hippo," she repeated, and put the comfort object down again. She peered at the unwrapped newchild, who waved his arms.

"I think newchildren are so cute," Lily sighed. "I hope I get **assign**ed to be a Birthmother."

"Lily!" Mother spoke very sharply. "Don't say that. There's very little honor in that Assignment."

"But I was talking to Natasha. You know the Ten who lives around the corner? She does some of her **volunteer** hours at the Birthing Center. And she told me that the Birthmothers get wonderful food, and they have very gentle exercise periods, and most of the time they just play games and **amuse** themselves while they're waiting. I think I'd like that," Lily said **petulant**ly.

"Three years," Mother told her firmly. "Three births, and that's all. After that they are Laborers for the rest of their adult lives, until the day that they enter the House of the Old. Is that what you want, Lily? Three lazy years, and then hard physical labor until you are old?"

"Well, no, I guess not," Lily **acknowledged** **reluctant**ly.

Father turned the newchild onto his **tummy** in the basket. He sat beside it and rubbed its small back with a rhythmic motion. "Anyway, Lily-billy," he said **affectionately**, "the Birthmothers never even get to see newchildren. If you enjoy the little ones so much, you should hope for an Assignment as Nurturer."

"When you're an Eight and start your volunteer hours, you can try some at the Nurturing Center," Mother suggested.

"Yes, I think I will," Lily said. She **knelt** beside the basket. "What did you say his name is? Gabriel? Hello, Gabriel," she said in a singsong voice. Then she giggled. "Ooops," she whispered. "I think he's asleep. I guess I'd better be quiet."

Jonas turned to the school assignments on his desk. Some chance of *that*, he thought. Lily was *never* quiet. Probably she should hope for an Assignment as Speaker, so that she could sit in the office with the microphone all day, making announcements. He laughed silently to himself, picturing his sister **droning** on in the **self-important** voice that all the Speakers seemed to develop, saying things like, ATTENTION. THIS IS A **REMINDER** TO FEMALES UNDER NINE THAT HAIR RIBBONS ARE TO BE **NEATLY** TIED AT ALL TIMES.

He turned toward Lily and noticed to his **satisfaction** that her ribbons were, as usual, undone and **dangling**. There would be an announcement like that quite soon, he felt certain, and it would be directed mainly at Lily, though her name, of course, would not be mentioned. Everyone would know.

Everyone had known, he remembered with **humiliation**, that the announcement ATTENTION. THIS IS A REMINDER TO MALE ELEVENS THAT OBJECTS ARE NOT TO BE REMOVED FROM THE RECREATION AREA AND THAT SNACKS ARE TO BE EATEN, NOT **HOARD**ED had been specifically directed at him, the day last month that he had taken an apple home. No one had mentioned it, not even his parents, because the public announcement had been **sufficient** to produce the **appropriate remorse**. He had, of course, **dispose**d of the apple and made his **apology** to the Recreation Director the next morning, before school.

Jonas thought again about that **incident**. He was still **bewilder**ed by it. Not by the announcement or the necessary apology; those were standard **procedure**s, and he had **deserve**d them—but by the incident itself. He probably should have brought up his feeling of bewilderment that very evening when the family unit had shared their feelings of the day. But he had not been able to sort out and put words to the source of his confusion, so he had let it pass.

It had happened during the recreation period, when he had been playing with Asher. Jonas had casually picked up an apple from the basket where the snacks were kept, and had thrown it to his friend. Asher had thrown it back, and they had begun a simple game of catch.

There had been nothing special about it; it was an activity that he had performed **countless** times: throw, catch; throw, catch. It was **effortless** for Jonas, and even boring, though Asher enjoyed it, and playing catch was a required activity for Asher because it would improve his hand-eye **coordination**, which was not up to standards.

But suddenly Jonas had noticed, following the path of the apple through the air with his eyes, that the piece of fruit had—well, this was the part that he couldn't **ade-quate**ly understand—the apple had *changed.* Just for an instant. It had changed in mid-air, he remembered. Then it was in his hand, and he looked at it carefully, but it was the same apple. Unchanged. The same size and shape: a perfect **sphere**. The same **nondescript** shade, about the same shade as his own **tunic**.

There was absolutely nothing **remarkable** about that apple. He had **toss**ed it back and forth between his hands a few times, then thrown it again to Asher. And again—in the air, for an instant only—it had changed.

It had happened four times. Jonas had **blink**ed, looked around, and then tested his **eyesight**, **squint**ing at the small print on the **identification** badge **attach**ed to his tunic. He read his name quite clearly. He could also clearly see Asher at the other end of the throwing area. And he had had no problem catching the apple.

Jonas had been completely **mystified**.

"Ash?" he had called. "Does anything seem strange to you? About the apple?"

"Yes," Asher called back, laughing. "It jumps out of my hand onto the ground!" Asher had just dropped it once again.

So Jonas laughed too, and with his laughter tried to **ignore** his uneasy **conviction** that *something* had happened. But he had taken the apple home, against the recreation area rules. That evening, before his parents and Lily arrived at the **dwelling**, he had held it in his hands and looked at it carefully. It was slightly **bruise**d now, because Asher had dropped it several times. But there was nothing at all unusual about the apple.

He had held a **magnifying glass** to it. He had tossed it several times across the room, watching, and then rolled it around and around on his desktop, waiting for the thing to happen again.

But it hadn't. The only thing that happened was the announcement later that evening over the speaker, the announcement that had singled him out without using his name, that had caused both of his parents to glance **meaningfull**y at his desk where the apple still lay.

Now, sitting at his desk, staring at his schoolwork as his family **hover**ed over the newchild in its basket, he shook his head, trying to forget the odd incident. He forced himself to arrange his papers and try to study a little before the evening meal. The newchild, Gabriel, **stir**red and **whimper**ed, and Father spoke softly to Lily, explaining the feeding procedure as he opened the container that held the **formula** and **equipment**.

The evening **proceed**ed as all evenings did in the family unit, in the dwelling, in the community: quiet, **reflective**, a time for **renewal** and preparation for the day to come. It was different only in the addition to it of the newchild with his pale, **solemn**, knowing eyes.

4

Jonas rode at a **leisurely** pace, glancing at the bikeports beside the buildings to see if he could **spot** Asher's. He didn't often do his volunteer hours with his friend because Asher frequently **fool**ed **around** and made serious work a little difficult. But now, with Twelve coming so soon and the volunteer hours ending, it didn't seem to matter.

The freedom to choose where to spend those hours had always seemed a wonderful **luxury** to Jonas; other hours of the day were so carefully **regulate**d.

He remembered when he had become an Eight, as Lily would do shortly, and had been faced with that freedom of choice. The Eights always set out on their first volunteer hour a little nervously, giggling and staying in groups of friends. They almost **invariably** did their hours on Recreation Duty first, helping with the younger ones in a place where they still felt comfortable. But with **guidance**, as they developed **self-confidence** and **maturity**, they moved on to other jobs, **gravitating** toward those that would suit their own interests and skills.

A male Eleven named Benjamin had done his entire nearly-Four years in the **Rehabilitation** Center, working with citizens who had been **injured**. It was **rumor**ed that he was as skilled now as the Rehabilitation Directors themselves, and that he had even developed some machines and methods to **hasten** rehabilitation. There was no doubt that Benjamin would receive his Assignment to that field and would probably be **permit**ted to **bypass** most of the training.

Jonas was **impress**ed by the things Benjamin had achieved. He knew him, of course, since they had always been groupmates, but they had never talked about the boy's **accomplish**ments because such a conversation would have been **awkward** for Benjamin. There was never any comfortable way to mention or discuss one's successes without breaking the rule against **brag**ging, even if one didn't mean to. It was a minor rule, rather like rudeness, **punishable** only by gentle **chastise**ment. But still. Better to **steer** clear of an **occasion** **govern**ed by a rule which would be so easy to break.

The area of dwellings behind him, Jonas rode past the community **structure**s, hoping to spot Asher's bicycle parked beside one of the small factories or office buildings. He passed the Childcare Center where Lily stayed after school, and the play areas surrounding it. He rode through the Central Plaza and the large **Auditorium** where public meetings were held.

Jonas slowed and looked at the **nametag**s on the bicycles lined up outside the Nurturing Center. Then he checked those outside Food **Distribution**; it was always fun to help with the deliveries, and he hoped he would find his friend there so that they could go together on the daily rounds, carrying the **carton**s of supplies into the dwellings of the community. But he finally found Asher's bicycle—leaning, as usual, instead of **upright** in its port, as it should have been—at the House of the Old.

There was only one other child's bicycle there, that of a female Eleven named Fiona. Jonas liked Fiona. She was a good student, quiet and polite, but she had a sense of fun as well, and it didn't surprise him that she was working with Asher today. He parked his bicycle neatly in the port beside theirs and entered the building.

"Hello, Jonas," the **attendant** at the front desk said. She handed him the sign-up sheet and stamped her own official **seal** beside his **signature**. All of his volunteer hours would be carefully **tabulated** at the Hall of Open Records. Once, long ago, it was whispered among the children, an Eleven had arrived at the Ceremony of Twelve only to hear a public announcement that he had not completed the required number of volunteer hours and would not, therefore, be given his Assignment. He had been permitted an additional month in which to complete the hours, and then given his Assignment privately, with no **applause**, no **celebration**: a **disgrace** that had **cloud**ed his entire future.

"It's good to have some volunteers here today," the attendant told him. "We **celebrate**d a release this morning, and that always throws the schedule off a little, so things get backed up." She looked at a printed sheet. "Let's see. Asher and Fiona are helping in the bathing room. Why don't you join them there? You know where it is, don't you?"

Jonas nodded, thanked her, and walked down the long hallway. He glanced into the rooms on either side. The Old were sitting quietly, some visiting and talking with one another, others doing handwork and simple **craft**s. A few were asleep. Each room was comfortably **furnish**ed, the floors covered with thick **carpeting**. It was a **serene** and slow-paced place, unlike the busy centers of manufacture and distribution where the daily work of the community occurred.

Jonas was glad that he had, over the years, chosen to do his hours in a variety of places so that he could experience the differences. He realized, though, that not focusing on one area meant he was left with not the slightest idea—not even a *guess*—of what his Assignment would be.

He laughed softly. Thinking about the Ceremony again, Jonas? He **teased** himself. But he **suspect**ed that with the date so near, probably all of his friends were, too.

He passed a **Caretaker** walking slowly with one of the Old in the hall. "Hello, Jonas," the young uniformed man said, smiling pleasantly. The woman beside him, whose arm he held, was **hunch**ed over as she **shuffle**d along in her soft slippers. She looked toward Jonas and smiled, but her dark eyes were clouded and **blank**. He realized she was **blind**.

He entered the bathing room with its warm **moist** air and **scent** of cleansing lotions. He removed his tunic, hung it carefully on a wall hook, and put on the volunteer's **smock** that was folded on a **shelf**.

"Hi, Jonas!" Asher called from the corner where he was **kneel**ing beside a **tub**. Jonas saw Fiona nearby, at a different tub. She looked up and smiled at him, but she was busy, gently washing a man who lay in the warm water.

Jonas greeted them and the caretaking attendants at work nearby. Then he went to the row of **padded lounging chair**s where others of the Old were waiting. He had worked here before; he knew what to do.

"Your turn, Larissa," he said, reading the nametag on the woman's **robe**. "I'll just start the water and then help you up." He pressed the button on a nearby empty tub and watched as the warm water flowed in through the many small openings on the sides. The tub would be filled in a minute and the water flow would stop automatically.

He helped the woman from the chair, led her to the tub, removed her robe, and **steadied** her with his hand on her arm as she stepped in and lowered herself. She leaned back and sighed with pleasure, her head on a soft **cushion**ed **headrest**.

"Comfortable?" he asked, and she nodded, her eyes closed. Jonas **squeeze**d cleansing lotion onto the clean sponge at the edge of the tub and began to wash her **frail** body.

Last night he had watched as his father **bath**ed the newchild. This was much the same: the **fragile** skin, the **soothing** water, the gentle motion of his hand, **slippery** with soap. The relaxed, peaceful smile on the woman's face reminded him of Gabriel being bathed.

And the **naked**ness, too. It was against the rules for children or adults to look at another's nakedness; but the rule did not apply to newchildren or the Old. Jonas was glad. It was a **nuisance** to keep oneself covered while changing for games, and the required apology if one had by mistake **glimpse**d another's body was always awkward. He couldn't see why it was necessary. He liked the feeling of safety here in this warm and quiet room; he liked the expression of trust on the woman's face as she lay in the water unprotected, exposed, and free.

From the corner of his eye he could see his friend Fiona help the old man from the tub and **tender**ly pat his thin, naked body dry with an **absorbent** cloth. She helped him into his robe.

Jonas thought Larissa had **drift**ed into sleep, as the Old often did, and he was careful to keep his motions steady and gentle so he wouldn't wake her. He was surprised when she spoke, her eyes still closed.

"This morning we celebrated the release of Roberto," she told him. "It was wonderful."

"I knew Roberto!" Jonas said. "I helped with his feeding the last time I was here, just a few weeks ago. He was a very interesting man."

Larissa opened her eyes happily. "They told his whole life before they released him," she said. "They always do. But to be honest," she whispered with a **mischievous** look, "some of the tellings are a little boring. I've even seen some of the Old fall asleep during tellings—when they released Edna recently. Did you know Edna?"

Jonas shook his head. He couldn't **recall** anyone named

Edna.

"Well, they tried to make her life sound **meaningful**. And of course," she added **primly**, "all lives *are* meaningful, I don't mean that they aren't. But *Edna*. My goodness. She was a Birthmother, and then she worked in Food Production for years, until she came here. She never even had a family unit."

Larissa lifted her head and looked around to make sure no one else was listening. Then she **confided**, "I don't think Edna was very smart."

Jonas laughed. He **rinsed** her left arm, **laid** it back into the water, and began to wash her feet. She **murmured** with pleasure as he massaged her feet with the sponge.

"But Roberto's life was wonderful," Larissa went on, after a moment. "He had been an Instructor of Elevens—you know how important that is—and he'd been on the Planning Committee. And—goodness, I don't know how he found the time—he also raised two very successful children, and he was *also* the one who did the landscaping design for the Central Plaza. He didn't do the actual labor, of course."

"Now your back. Lean forward and I'll help you sit up." Jonas put his arm around her and supported her as she sat. He squeezed the sponge against her back and began to rub her sharp-boned shoulders. "Tell me about the celebration."

"Well, there was the telling of his life. That is always first. Then the **toast**. We all raised our glasses and cheered. We **chanted** the **anthem**. He made a lovely good-bye speech. And several of us made little speeches wishing him well. I didn't, though. I've never been **fond** of public speaking.

"He was **thrilled**. You should have seen the look on his face when they let him go."

Jonas slowed the strokes of his hand on her back thoughtfully. "Larissa," he asked, "what happens when they make the actual release? Where exactly did Roberto go?"

She lifted her **bare** wet shoulders in a small shrug. "I don't know. I don't think anybody does, except the committee. He just **bowed** to all of us and then walked, like they all do, through the special door in the Releasing Room. But you should have seen his look. Pure happiness, I'd call it."

Jonas grinned. "I wish I'd been there to see it."

Larissa **frowned**. "I don't know why they don't let children come. Not enough room, I guess. They should **enlarge** the Releasing Room."

"We'll have to suggest that to the committee. Maybe they'd study it," Jonas said **slyly**, and Larissa **chortled** with laughter.

"*Right!*" she **hooted**, and Jonas helped her from the tub.

5

Usually, at the morning **ritual** when the family members told their dreams, Jonas didn't **contribute** much. He **rare**ly dreamed. Sometimes he awoke with a feeling of **fragment**s **afloat** in his sleep, but he couldn't seem to **grasp** them and put them together into something worthy of telling at the ritual.

But this morning was different. He had dreamed very **vivid**ly the night before.

His mind **wander**ed while Lily, as usual, **recount**ed a **lengthy** dream, this one a **frighten**ing one in which she had, against the rules, been riding her mother's bicycle and been caught by the Security Guards.

They all listened carefully and discussed with Lily the warning that the dream had given.

"Thank you for your dream, Lily." Jonas said the standard

phrase automatically, and tried to pay better attention while his mother told of a dream fragment, a **disquiet**ing scene where she had been chastised for a rule **infraction** she didn't understand. Together they agreed that it probably resulted from her feelings when she had **reluctant**ly dealt **punish**ment to the citizen who had broken the major rules a second time.

Father said that he had had no dreams.

"Gabe?" Father asked, looking down at the basket where the newchild lay **gurgling** after his feeding, ready to be taken back to the **Nurturing** Center for the day.

They all laughed. Dream-telling began with Threes. If newchildren dreamed, no one knew.

"Jonas?" Mother asked. They always asked, though they knew how rarely Jonas had a dream to tell.

"I *did* dream last night," Jonas told them. He **shift**ed in his chair, frowning.

"Good," Father said. "Tell us."

"The details aren't clear, really," Jonas explained, trying to **recreate** the odd dream in his mind. "I think I was in the bathing room at the House of the Old."

"That's where you were yesterday," Father pointed out.

Jonas nodded. "But it wasn't really the same. There was a **tub**, in the dream. But only one. And the real bathing room has rows and rows of them. But the room in the dream was warm and **damp**. And I had taken off my tunic, but hadn't put on the **smock**, so my **chest** was **bare**. I was **perspiring**, because it was so warm. And Fiona was there, the way she was yesterday."

"Asher, too?" Mother asked.

Jonas shook his head. "No. It was only me and Fiona, alone in the room, standing beside the tub. She was laughing. But I wasn't. I was almost a little angry at her, in the dream, because she wasn't taking me seriously."

"Seriously about what?" Lily asked.

Jonas looked at his plate. For some reason that he didn't understand, he felt slightly **embarrassed**. "I think I was trying to **convince** her that she should get into the tub of water."

He paused. He knew he had to tell it all, that it was not only all right but necessary to tell *all* of a dream. So he forced himself to relate the part that made him uneasy.

"I wanted her to take off her clothes and get into the tub," he explained quickly. "I wanted to **bathe** her. I had the sponge in my hand. But she wouldn't. She kept laughing and saying no."

He looked up at his parents. "That's all," he said.

"Can you describe the strongest feeling in your dream, son?" Father asked.

Jonas thought about it. The details were **murky** and

vague. But the feelings were clear, and **flood**ed him again now as he thought. "The *wanting*," he said. "I knew that she wouldn't. And I think I knew that she *shouldn't*. But I wanted it so terribly. I could feel the wanting all through me."

"Thank you for your dream, Jonas," Mother said after a moment. She glanced at Father.

"Lily," Father said, "it's time to leave for school. Would you walk beside me this morning and **keep an eye on** the newchild's basket? We want to be certain he doesn't **wiggle** himself loose."

Jonas began to rise to collect his schoolbooks. He thought it surprising that they hadn't talked about his dream **at length** before the thank you. Perhaps they found it as confusing as he had.

"Wait, Jonas," Mother said gently. "I'll write an apology to your instructor so that you won't have to speak one for being late."

He **sank** back down into his chair, **puzzled**. He waved to Father and Lily as they left the dwelling, carrying Gabe in his basket. He watched while Mother **tidied** the remains of the morning meal and placed the **tray** by the front door for the Collection Crew.

Finally she sat down beside him at the table. "Jonas," she said with a smile, "the feeling you described as the wanting?

It was your first **Stirrings**. Father and I have been expecting it to happen to you. It happens to everyone. It happened to Father when he was your age. And it happened to me. It will happen someday to Lily.

"And very often," Mother added, "it begins with a dream."

Stirrings. He had heard the word before. He remembered that there was a **reference** to the Stirrings in the Book of Rules, though he didn't remember what it said. And **now and then** the Speaker mentioned it. ATTENTION. A **REMINDER** THAT STIRRINGS MUST BE REPORTED IN ORDER FOR **TREATMENT** TO **TAKE PLACE**.

He had always **ignore**d that announcement because he didn't understand it and it had never seemed to apply to him in any way. He ignored, as most citizens did, many of the commands and reminders read by the Speaker.

"Do I have to report it?" he asked his mother.

She laughed. "You did, in the dream-telling. That's enough."

"But what about the treatment? The Speaker says that treatment must take place." Jonas felt **miserable**. Just when the **Ceremony** was about to happen, his Ceremony of Twelve, would he have to go away someplace for treatment? Just because of a stupid dream?

But his mother laughed again in a **reassuring**, affectionate way. "No, no," she said. "It's just the **pill**s. You're ready for the pills, that's all. That's the treatment for Stirrings."

Jonas **brighten**ed. He knew about the pills. His parents both took them each morning. And some of his friends did, he knew. Once he had been heading off to school with Asher, both of them on their bikes, when Asher's father had called from their dwelling doorway, "You forgot your pill, Asher!" Asher had **groan**ed **good-natured**ly, turned his bike, and ridden back while Jonas waited.

It was the sort of thing one didn't ask a friend about because it might have fallen into that uncomfortable category of "being different." Asher took a pill each morning; Jonas did not. Always better, less rude, to talk about things that were the same.

Now he **swallow**ed the small pill that his mother handed him.

"That's all?" he asked.

"That's all," she replied, returning the bottle to the **cupboard**. "But you mustn't forget. I'll remind you for the first weeks, but then you must do it on your own. If you forget, the Stirrings will come back. The dreams of Stirrings will come back. Sometimes the **dosage** must be **adjust**ed."

"Asher takes them," Jonas **confide**d.

His mother nodded, unsurprised. "Many of your groupmates probably do. The males, at least. And they all will, soon. Females too."

"How long will I have to take them?"

"Until you enter the House of the Old," she explained. "All of your adult life. But it becomes routine; after a while you won't even pay much attention to it."

She looked at her watch. "If you leave right now, you won't even be late for school. Hurry along.

"And thank you again, Jonas," she added, as he went to the door, "for your dream."

Pedaling rapidly down the path, Jonas felt oddly proud to have joined those who took the pills. For a moment, though, he remembered the dream again. The dream had felt **pleasurable**. Though the feelings were confused, he thought that he had liked the feelings that his mother had called Stirrings. He remembered that upon waking, he had wanted to feel the Stirrings again.

Then, in the same way that his own dwelling **slipped** away behind him as he rounded a corner on his bicycle, the dream slipped away from his thoughts. Very briefly, a little **guiltily**, he tried to grasp it back. But the feelings had disappeared. The Stirrings were gone.

6

"Lily, *please* hold still," Mother said again.

Lily, standing in front of her, **fidget**ed **impatient**ly. "I can tie them myself," she complained. "I always have."

"I know that," Mother replied, **straighten**ing the hair ribbons on the little girl's **braid**s. "But I also know that they constantly come loose and **more often than not**, they're **dangling** down your back by afternoon. Today, at least, we want them to be **neat**ly tied and to *stay* neatly tied."

"I don't like hair ribbons. I'm glad I only have to wear them one more year," Lily said **irritably**. "Next year I get my bicycle, too," she added more cheerfully.

"There are good things each year," Jonas reminded her. "This year you get to start your **volunteer** hours. And remember last year, when you became a Seven, you were so happy to get your front-buttoned jacket?"

The little girl nodded and looked down at herself, at the jacket with its row of large buttons that **designate**d her as a Seven. Fours, Fives, and Sixes all wore jackets that **fasten**ed down the back so that they would have to help each other dress and would learn **interdependence**.

The front-buttoned jacket was the first sign of independence, the first very visible symbol of growing up. The bicycle, at Nine, would be the powerful **emblem** of moving **graduall**y out into the community, away from the **protective** family unit.

Lily **grin**ned and **wriggle**d away from her mother. "And this year you get your **Assign**ment," she said to Jonas in an excited voice. "I hope you get Pilot. And that you take me flying!"

"Sure I will," said Jonas. "And I'll get a special little **parachute** that just fits you, and I'll take you up to, oh, maybe twenty thousand feet, and open the door, and—"

"*Jonas*," Mother warned.

"I was only joking," Jonas **groan**ed. "I don't want Pilot, anyway. If I get Pilot I'll put in an **appeal**."

"Come on," Mother said. She gave Lily's ribbons a final **tug**. "Jonas? Are you ready? Did you take your **pill**? I want to get a good seat in the **Auditorium**." She **prod**ded Lily to the front door and Jonas followed.

It was a short ride to the Auditorium, Lily waving to

her friends from her seat on the back of Mother's bicycle. Jonas **stow**ed his bicycle beside Mother's and made his way through the **throng** to find his group.

The entire community attended the Ceremony each year. For the parents, it meant two days holiday from work; they sat together in the huge hall. Children sat with their groups until they went, one by one, to the stage.

Father, though, would not join Mother in the audience right away. For the earliest ceremony, the Naming, the Nurturers brought the newchildren to the stage. Jonas, from his place in the balcony with the Elevens, searched the Auditorium for a **glimpse** of Father. It wasn't at all hard to **spot** the Nurturers' section at the front; coming from it were the **wail**s and **howl**s of the newchildren who sat **squirm**ing on the Nurturers' **lap**s. At every other public ceremony, the audience was silent and **attentive**. But once a year, they all smiled **indulgent**ly at the **commotion** from the little ones waiting to receive their names and families.

Jonas finally caught his father's eye and waved. Father grinned and waved back, then held up the hand of the newchild on his lap, making it wave, too.

It wasn't Gabriel. Gabe was back at the Nurturing Center today, being cared for by the night crew. He had been given an unusual and special **reprieve** from the **committee**, and **grant**ed an additional year of nurturing before his Naming and **Placement**. Father had gone before the committee with a **plea** on behalf of Gabriel, who had not yet gained the weight **appropriate** to his days of life nor begun to **sleep soundly** enough at night to be placed with his family unit. Normally such a newchild would be **label**ed **Inadequate** and **release**d from the community.

Instead, as a result of Father's plea, Gabriel had been labeled Uncertain and given the additional year. He would continue to be nurtured at the Center and would spend his nights with Jonas's family unit. Each family member, including Lily, had been required to sign a **pledge** that they would not become **attach**ed to this little **temporary** guest, and that they would **relinquish** him without **protest** or appeal when he was assigned to his own family unit at next year's Ceremony.

At least, Jonas thought, after Gabriel was placed next year, they would still see him often because he would be part of the community. If he were released, they would not see him again. Ever. Those who were released—even as newchildren—were sent Elsewhere and never returned to the community.

Father had not had to release a single newchild this year, so Gabriel would have **represent**ed a real failure and sadness. Even Jonas, though he didn't **hover** over the little one the way Lily and his father did, was glad that Gabe had not been released.

The first Ceremony began right on time, and Jonas watched as one after another each newchild was given a name and handed by the Nurturers to its new family unit. For some, it was a first child. But many came to the stage **accompanied** by another child **beam**ing with pride to receive a little brother or sister, the way Jonas had when he was about to be a Five.

Asher **poke**d Jonas's arm. "Remember when we got Phillipa?" he asked in a loud whisper. Jonas nodded. It had only been last year. Asher's parents had waited quite a long time before applying for a second child. Maybe, Jonas **sus-pect**ed, they had been so **exhaust**ed by Asher's **lively** foolish-ness that they had needed a little time.

Two of their group, Fiona and another female named Thea, were missing temporarily, waiting with their parents to receive newchildren. But it was rare that there was such an age gap between children in a family unit.

When her family's ceremony was completed, Fiona took the seat that had been saved for her in the row ahead of Asher and Jonas. She turned and whispered to them, "He's cute. But I don't like his name very much." She **made a face** and **giggle**d. Fiona's new brother had been named Bruno. It wasn't a *great* name, Jonas thought, like—well, like Gabriel, for example. But it was okay.

The audience **applause**, which was **enthusiastic** at each Naming, rose in an **exuberant swell** when one parental pair, **glow**ing with pride, took a male newchild and heard him named Caleb.

This new Caleb was a replacement child. The couple had lost their first Caleb, a cheerful little Four. Loss of a child was very, very rare. The community was **extraordinarily** safe, each citizen watchful and protective of all children. But somehow the first little Caleb had **wander**ed away unnoticed, and had fallen into the river. The entire community had performed the Ceremony of Loss together, murmuring the name Caleb throughout an entire day, less and less frequently, softer in volume, as the long and **somber** day went on, so that the little Four seemed to fade away gradually from everyone's consciousness.

Now, at this special Naming, the community performed the brief Murmur-of-Replacement Ceremony, repeating the name for the first time since the loss: softly and slowly at first, then faster and with greater volume, as the couple stood on the stage with the newchild sleeping in the mother's arms. It was as if the first Caleb were returning.

Another newchild was given the name Roberto, and Jonas remembered that Roberto the Old had been released only last week. But there was no Murmur-of-Replacement Ceremony for the new little Roberto. Release was not the same as Loss.

He sat politely through the ceremonies of Two and Three and Four, increasingly bored as he was each year. Then a break for **midday** meal—served outdoors—and back again to the seats, for the Fives, Sixes, Sevens, and finally, last of the first day's ceremonies, the Eights.

Jonas watched and cheered as Lily **march**ed proudly to the stage, became an Eight and received the identifying jacket that she would wear this year, this one with smaller buttons and, for the first time, pockets, indicating that she was **mature** enough now to **keep track of** her own small **belong**ings. She stood **solemn**ly listening to the speech of firm instructions on the responsibilities of Eight and doing volunteer hours for the first time. But Jonas could see that Lily, though she seemed attentive, was looking **longing**ly at the row of **gleam**ing bicycles, which would be presented tomorrow morning to the Nines.

Next year, Lily-billy, Jonas thought.

It was an exhausting day, and even Gabriel, **retrieve**d in his basket from the Nurturing Center, slept soundly that night.

Finally it was the morning of the Ceremony of Twelve.

Now Father sat beside Mother in the audience. Jonas could see them **applaud**ing **dutiful**ly as the Nines, one by one, wheeled their new bicycles, each with its gleaming **nametag** attached to the back, from the stage. He knew that his parents **cringe**d a little, as he did, when Fritz, who lived in the dwelling next door to theirs, received his bike and almost immediately **bump**ed into the **podium** with it. Fritz was a very **awkward** child who had been **summon**ed for chastisement again and again. His **transgression**s were small ones, always: shoes on the wrong feet, schoolwork misplaced, failure to study **adequate**ly for a quiz. But each such error **reflect**ed negatively on his parents' **guidance** and **infringe**d on the community's sense of order and success. Jonas and his family had not been looking forward to Fritz's bicycle, which they realized would probably too often be dropped on the front walk instead of wheeled neatly into its **port**.

Finally the Nines were all **resettle**d in their seats, each having wheeled a bicycle outside where it would be waiting for its owner at the end of the day. Everyone always **chuckle**d and made small jokes when the Nines rode home for the first time. "Want me to show you how to ride?" older friends would call. "I know you've never been on a bike before!" But **invariably** the grinning Nines, who in technical **violation** of the rule had been practicing secretly for weeks, would **mount** and ride off in perfect balance, training wheels never touching the ground.

Then the Tens. Jonas never found the Ceremony of Ten particularly interesting—only time-consuming, as each child's hair was **snip**ped neatly into its **distinguish**ing cut: females lost their braids at Ten, and males, too, relinquished their long childish hair and took on the more manly short style which exposed their ears.

Laborers moved quickly to the stage with **broom**s and swept away the **mound**s of **discard**ed hair. Jonas could see the parents of the new Tens **stir** and murmur, and he knew that this evening, in many **dwelling**s, they would be snipping and straightening the **hastily** done haircuts, **trim**ming them into a neater line.

Elevens. It seemed a short time ago that Jonas had undergone the Ceremony of Eleven, but he remembered that it was not one of the more interesting ones. By Eleven, one was only waiting to be Twelve. It was simply a marking of time with no meaningful changes. There was new clothing: different **undergarment**s for the females, whose bodies were beginning to change; and longer **trousers** for the males, with a specially shaped pocket for the small **calculator** that they would use this year in school; but those were simply presented in wrapped packages without an accompanying speech.

Break for midday meal. Jonas realized he was hungry. He and his groupmates **congregate**d by the tables in front of the Auditorium and took their packaged food. Yesterday there had been **merriment** at lunch, a lot of teasing and energy. But today the group stood **anxiously**, separate from the other children. Jonas watched the new Nines **gravitate** toward their waiting bicycles, each one admiring his or her nametag. He saw the Tens **stroking** their new shortened hair, the females shaking their heads to feel the **unaccustomed** lightness without the heavy braids they had worn so long.

"I heard about a guy who was absolutely certain he was going to be assigned Engineer," Asher **mutter**ed as they ate, "and instead they gave him **Sanitation** Laborer. He went out the next day, jumped into the river, swam across, and joined the next community he came to. Nobody ever saw him again."

Jonas laughed. "Somebody made that story up, Ash," he said. "My father said he heard that story when *he* was a Twelve."

But Asher wasn't reassured. He was eyeing the river where it was visible behind the Auditorium. "I can't even swim very well," he said. "My swimming instructor said that I don't have the right **boyish**ness or something."

"**Buoyancy**," Jonas corrected him.

"Whatever. I don't have it. I sink."

"Anyway," Jonas pointed out, "have you ever once

known of anyone—I mean really known for sure, Asher, not just heard a story about it—who joined another community?"

"No," Asher admitted reluctantly. "But you can. It says so in the rules. If you don't fit in, you can apply for Elsewhere and be released. My mother says that once, about ten years ago, someone applied and was gone the next day." Then he chuckled. "She told me that because I was driving her crazy. She threatened to apply for Elsewhere."

"She was joking."

"I know. But it was true, what she said, that someone did that once. She said that it was really true. Here today and gone tomorrow. Never seen again. Not even a Ceremony of Release."

Jonas **shrugged**. It didn't worry him. How could someone not fit in? The community was so **meticulous**ly ordered, the choices so carefully made.

Even the Matching of **Spouse**s was given such **weighty** consideration that sometimes an adult who applied to receive a spouse waited months or even *years* before a Match was **approved** and announced. All of the factors—**disposition**, energy level, intelligence, and interests—had to **correspond** and to **interact** perfectly. Jonas's mother, for example, had higher intelligence than his father; but his father had a calmer disposition. They balanced each other.

Their Match, which like all Matches had been monitored by the Committee of **Elders** for three years before they could apply for children, had always been a successful one.

Like the Matching of Spouses and the Naming and Placement of newchildren, the Assignments were **scrupulously** thought through by the Committee of Elders.

He was certain that his Assignment, whatever it was to be, and Asher's too, would be the right one for them. He only wished that the midday break would conclude, that the audience would **reenter** the Auditorium, and the **suspense** would end.

As if in answer to his unspoken wish, the signal came and the crowd began to move toward the doors.

7

Now Jonas's group had taken a new place in the Auditorium, trading with the new Elevens, so that they sat in the very front, immediately before the stage.

They were arranged by their original numbers, the numbers they had been given at birth. The numbers were rarely used after the Naming. But each child knew his number, of course. Sometimes parents used them in **irritation** at a child's **misbehavior**, indicating that **mischief** made one **unworthy** of a name. Jonas always **chuckle**d when he heard a parent, **exasperate**d, call sharply to a **whining toddler**, "That's *enough*, Twenty-three!"

Jonas was Nineteen. He had been the nineteenth newchild born his year. It had meant that at his Naming, he had been already standing and bright-eyed, soon to walk and talk. It had given him a slight advantage the first year or two, a little more **maturity** than many of his groupmates who had been born in the later months of that year. But it **evened out**, as it always did, by Three.

After Three, the children **progressed** at much the same level, though by their first number one could always tell who was a few months older than others in his group. **Technically**, Jonas's full number was Eleven-nineteen, since there were other Nineteens, of course, in each age group. And today, now that the new Elevens had been advanced this morning, there were *two* Eleven-nineteens. At the midday break he had exchanged smiles with the new one, a shy female named Harriet.

But the **duplication** was only for these few hours. Very soon he would not be an Eleven but a Twelve, and age would no longer matter. He would be an adult, like his parents, though a new one and untrained still.

Asher was Four, and sat now in the row ahead of Jonas. He would receive his Assignment fourth.

Fiona, Eighteen, was on his left; on his other side sat Twenty, a male named Pierre whom Jonas didn't like much. Pierre was very serious, not much fun, and a **worrier** and **tattletale**, too. "Have you checked the rules, Jonas?" Pierre was always whispering solemnly. "I'm not sure that's within the rules." Usually it was some foolish thing that no one cared about—opening his **tunic** if it was a day with a

breeze; taking a brief try on a friend's bicycle, just to experience the different feel of it.

The **initial** speech at the Ceremony of Twelve was made by the Chief Elder, the leader of the community who was **elect**ed every ten years. The speech was much the same each year: **recollection** of the time of childhood and the period of preparation, the coming responsibilities of adult life, the **profound** importance of Assignment, the seriousness of training to come.

Then the Chief Elder moved ahead in her speech.

"This is the time," she began, looking directly at them, when we **acknowledge** differences. You Elevens have spent all your years till now learning to fit in, to **standardize** your behavior, to **curb** any **impulse** that might set you apart from the group.

"But today we honor your differences. They have **determine**d your futures."

She began to describe this year's group and its variety of personalities, though she singled no one out by name. She mentioned that there was one who had singular skills at caretaking, another who loved newchildren, one with unusual scientific **aptitude**, and a fourth for whom physical labor was an obvious pleasure. Jonas **shift**ed in his seat, trying to recognize each **reference** as one of his groupmates. The caretaking skills were no doubt those of Fiona, on his left; he remembered noticing the **tender**ness with which she had bathed the Old. Probably the one with scientific aptitude was Benjamin, the male who had **devise**d new, important **equipment** for the **Rehabilitation** Center.

He heard nothing that he recognized as himself, Jonas.

Finally the Chief Elder paid **tribute** to the hard work of her committee, which had performed the **observation**s so **meticulous**ly all year. The Committee of Elders stood and was acknowledged by applause. Jonas noticed Asher **yawn** slightly, covering his mouth politely with his hand.

Then, at last, the Chief Elder called number One to the stage, and the Assignments began.

Each announcement was **lengthy**, **accompanied** by a speech directed at the new Twelve. Jonas tried to pay attention as One, smiling happily, received her Assignment as Fish **Hatchery Attendant** along with words of **praise** for her childhood spent doing many volunteer hours there, and her obvious interest in the important process of providing **nourishment** for the community.

Number One—her name was Madeline—returned, finally, **amidst** applause, to her seat, wearing the new badge that **designate**d her Fish Hatchery Attendant. Jonas was certainly glad that *that* Assignment was taken; he wouldn't have wanted it. But he gave Madeline a smile of congratulation.

When Two, a female named Inger, received her Assignment as Birthmother, Jonas remembered that his mother had called it a job without honor. But he thought that the Committee had chosen well. Inger was a nice girl though somewhat lazy, and her body was strong. She would enjoy the three years of being **pamper**ed that would follow her brief training; she would give birth easily and well; and the task of Laborer that would follow would use her strength, keep her healthy, and **impose** self-**discipline**. Inger was smiling when she **resume**d her seat. Birthmother was an important job, if lacking in **prestige**.

Jonas noticed that Asher looked nervous. He kept turning his head and **glancing** back at Jonas until the group leader had to give him a silent **chastise**ment, a motion to sit still and face forward.

Three, Isaac, was given an Assignment as Instructor of Sixes, which obviously pleased him and was well **deserve**d. Now there were three Assignments gone, none of them ones that Jonas would have liked—not that he could have been a Birthmother, anyway, he realized with **amuse**ment. He tried to sort through the list in his mind, the possible Assignments that remained. But there were so many he gave it up; and anyway, now it was Asher's turn. He paid strict attention as his friend went to the stage and stood **self-consciousl**y beside the Chief Elder.

"All of us in the community know and enjoy Asher," the Chief Elder began. Asher grinned and scratched one leg with the other foot. The audience chuckled softly.

"When the committee began to consider Asher's Assignment," she went on, "there were some possibilities that were immediately **discard**ed. Some that would clearly, not have been right for Asher.

"For example," she said, smiling, "we did not consider for an instant designating Asher an Instructor of Threes."

The audience **howl**ed with laughter. Asher laughed, too, looking **sheepish** but pleased at the special attention. The Instructors of Threes were in charge of the **acquisition** of correct language.

"In fact," the Chief Elder continued, chuckling a little herself, "we even gave a little thought to some **retroactive** chastisement for the one who had been *Asher's* Instructor of Threes so long ago. At the meeting where Asher was discussed, we retold many of the stories that we all remembered from his days of language acquisition.

"Especially," she said, chuckling, "the difference between snack and **smack**. Remember, Asher?"

Asher nodded **ruefully**, and the audience laughed aloud. Jonas did, too. He remembered, though he had been only a Three at the time himself.

The punishment used for small children was a **regulate**d

system of smacks with the discipline **wand**: a thin, **flexible** weapon that **stung** painfully when it was **wield**ed. The Childcare specialists were trained very carefully in the discipline methods: a quick smack across the hands for a bit of minor misbehavior; three sharper smacks on the **bare** legs for a second **offense**.

Poor Asher, who always talked too fast and mixed up words, even as a toddler. As a Three, **eager** for his juice and crackers at snacktime, he one day said "smack" instead of "snack" as he stood waiting in line for the morning **treat**.

Jonas remembered it clearly. He could still see little Asher, wiggling with impatience in the line. He remembered the cheerful voice call out, "I want my smack!"

The other Threes, including Jonas, had laughed nervously. "Snack!" they corrected. "You meant snack, Asher!" But the mistake had been made. And **precision** of language was one of the most important tasks of small children. Asher had asked for a smack.

The discipline wand, in the hand of the Childcare worker, whistled as it came down across Asher's hands. Asher **whimpere**d, **cringe**d, and corrected himself instantly. "Snack," he whispered.

But the next morning he had done it again. And again the following week. He couldn't seem to stop, though for each **lapse** the discipline wand came again, **escalating** to a series of painful **lash**es that left marks on Asher's legs. **Eventually**, for a period of time, Asher stopped talking altogether, when he was a Three.

"For a while," the Chief Elder said, relating the story, "we had a silent Asher! But he learned."

She turned to him with a smile. "When he began to talk again, it was with greater precision. And now his lapses are very few. His corrections and apologies are very **prompt**. And his good humor is **unfailing**." The audience **mur-mur**ed in agreement. Asher's cheerful **disposition** was well-known throughout the community.

"Asher." She lifted her voice to make the official announcement. "We have given you the Assignment of Assistant Director of Recreation."

She clipped on his new badge as he stood beside her, **beam**ing. Then he turned and left the stage as the audience cheered. When he had taken his seat again, the Chief Elder looked down at him and said the words that she had said now four times, and would say to each new Twelve. Somehow she gave it special meaning for each of them.

"Asher, " she said, "thank you for your childhood."

The Assignments continued, and Jonas watched and listened, **relieved** now by the wonderful Assignment his best friend had been given. But he was more and more **appre-**

hensive as his own approached. Now the new Twelves in the row ahead had all received their badges. They were **fingering** them as they sat, and Jonas knew that each one was thinking about the training that lay ahead. For some—one **studious** male had been selected as Doctor, a female as Engineer, and another for Law and **Justice**—it would be years of hard work and study. Others, like Laborers and Birthmothers, would have a much shorter training period.

Eighteen, Fiona, on his left, was called. Jonas knew she must be nervous, but Fiona was a calm female. She had been sitting quietly, **serenely**, throughout the Ceremony.

Even the applause, though **enthusiastic**, seemed serene when Fiona was given the important Assignment of **Caretaker** of the Old. It was perfect for such a sensitive, gentle girl, and her smile was satisfied and pleased when she took her seat beside him again.

Jonas prepared himself to walk to the stage when the applause ended and the Chief Elder picked up the next folder and looked down to the group to call forward the next new Twelve. He was calm now that his turn had come. He took a deep breath and smoothed his hair with his hand.

"Twenty," he heard her voice say clearly. "Pierre."

She skipped me, Jonas thought, **stun**ned. Had he heard wrong? No. There was a sudden **hush** in the crowd, and he knew that the entire community realized that the Chief Elder had moved from Eighteen to Twenty, leaving a gap. On his right, Pierre, with a **startle**d look, rose from his seat and moved to the stage.

A mistake. She made a mistake. But Jonas knew, even as he had the thought, that she hadn't. The Chief Elder made no mistakes. Not at the Ceremony of Twelve.

He felt **dizzy**, and couldn't focus his attention. He didn't hear what Assignment Pierre received, and was only **dim**ly aware of the applause as the boy returned, wearing his new badge. Then: Twenty-one. Twenty-two.

The numbers continued in order. Jonas sat, **daze**d, as they moved into the Thirties and then the Forties, nearing the end. Each time, at each announcement, his heart jumped for a moment, and he thought wild thoughts. Perhaps now she would call his name. Could he have forgotten his own number? No. He had always been Nineteen. He was sitting in the seat marked Nineteen.

But she had *skipped* him. He saw the others in his group glance at him, embarrassed, and then **avert** their eyes quickly. He saw a worried look on the face of his group leader.

He **hunch**ed his shoulders and tried to make himself smaller in the seat. He wanted to disappear, to fade away, not to exist. He didn't dare to turn and find his parents in the crowd. He couldn't bear to see their faces darkened with **shame**.

Jonas **bow**ed his head and searched through his mind. *What had he done wrong*?

8

The audience was clearly **ill at ease**. They **applaud**ed at the final Assignment; but the applause was **piecemeal**, no longer a **crescendo** of united enthusiasm. There were murmurs of confusion.

Jonas moved his hands together, **clapping**, but it was an automatic, meaningless gesture that he wasn't even aware of. His mind had shut out all of the earlier emotions: the **anticipation**, excitement, pride, and even the happy **kinship** with his friends. Now he felt only **humiliation** and terror.

The Chief Elder waited until the uneasy applause **subsided**. Then she spoke again.

"I know," she said in her **vibrant**, **gracious** voice, "that you are all concerned. That you feel I have made a mistake."

She smiled. The community, **relieve**d from its **discom-**

fort very slightly by her **benign** statement, seemed to breathe more easily. It was very silent.

Jonas looked up.

"I have caused you **anxiety**," she said. "I **apologize** to my community." Her voice flowed over the **assemble**d crowd.

"We accept your **apology**," they all **utter**ed together.

"Jonas," she said, looking down at him, "I apologize to you in particular. I caused you **anguish**."

"I accept your apology," Jonas replied shakily.

"Please come to the stage now."

Earlier that day, dressing in his own dwelling, he had practiced the kind of **jaunty**, **self-assured** walk that he hoped he could make to the stage when his turn came. All of that was forgotten now. He simply **will**ed himself to stand, to move his feet that felt **weighted** and **clumsy**, to go forward, up the steps and across the platform until he stood at her side.

Reassuringly she placed her arm across his tense shoulders.

"Jonas has not been assigned," she informed the crowd, and his heart **sank**.

Then she went on. "Jonas has been *selected*."

He **blink**ed. What did that mean? He felt a **collective**, **questioning** stir from the audience. They, too, were **puzzle**d.

In a firm, commanding voice she announced, "Jonas has been selected to be our next Receiver of Memory."

Then he heard the **gasp**—the sudden **intake** of breath, drawn sharply in **astonish**ment, by each of the seated citizens. He saw their faces; the eyes widened in **awe**.

And still he did not understand.

"Such a selection is very, very **rare**," the Chief Elder told the audience. "Our community has only one Receiver. It is he who trains his **successor**.

"We have had our current Receiver for a very long time," she went on. Jonas followed her eyes and saw that she was looking at one of the Elders. The Committee of Elders was sitting together in a group; and the Chief Elder's eyes were now on one who sat in the midst but seemed oddly separate from them. It was a man Jonas had never noticed before, a **beard**ed man with pale eyes. He was watching Jonas **intent**ly.

"We failed in our last selection," the Chief Elder said solemnly. "It was ten years ago, when Jonas was just a **toddler**. I will not **dwell** on the experience because it causes us all terrible discomfort."

Jonas didn't know what she was referring to, but he could sense the discomfort of the audience. They shifted uneasily in their seats.

"We have not been **hasty** this time," she continued.

"We could not afford another failure."

"Sometimes," she went on, speaking now in a lighter tone, relaxing the **tension** in the Auditorium, "we are not entirely certain about the Assignments, even after the most **painstaking observations**. Sometimes we worry that the one assigned might not develop, through training, every **attribute** necessary. Elevens are still children, after all. What we **observe** as playfulness and **patience**—the requirements to become **Nurturer**—could, with maturity, be **reveal**ed as simply foolishness and **indolence**. So we continue to observe during training, and to **modify** behavior when necessary.

"But the Receiver-in-training cannot be observed, cannot be modified. That is stated quite clearly in the rules. He is to be alone, apart, while he is prepared by the current Receiver for the job which is the most honored in our community."

Alone? Apart? Jonas listened with increasing unease.

"Therefore the selection must be sound. It must be a **unanimous** choice of the Committee. They can have no doubts, however **fleeting**. If, during the process, an Elder reports a dream of uncertainty, that dream has the power to set a **candidate** aside instantly.

"Jonas was identified as a possible Receiver many years ago. We have observed him meticulously. There were no dreams of uncertainty.

"He has shown all of the qualities that a Receiver must have."

With her hand still firmly on his shoulder, the Chief Elder listed the qualities.

"Intelligence," she said. "We are all aware that Jonas has been a top student throughout his school days.

"Integrity," she said next. "Jonas has, like all of us, committed minor transgressions." She smiled at him. "We expect that. We hoped, also, that he would present himself **prompt**ly for chastisement, and he has always done so.

"Courage," she went on. "Only one of us here today has ever undergone the **rigorous** training required of a Receiver. He, of course, is the most important member of the Committee: the current Receiver. It was he who reminded us, again and again, of the courage required.

"Jonas," she said, turning to him, but speaking in a voice that the entire community could hear, "the training required of you **involve**s pain. Physical pain."

He felt fear **flutter** within him.

"You have never experienced that. Yes, you have **scrape**d your knees in falls from your bicycle. Yes, you **crush**ed your finger in a door last year."

Jonas nodded, agreeing, as he **recall**ed the **incident**, and its **accompany**ing **misery**.

"But you will be faced, now," she explained gently, "with pain of a **magnitude** that none of us here can **comprehend** because it is beyond our experience. The Receiver himself was not able to describe it, only to remind us that you would be faced with it, that you would need **immense** courage. We cannot prepare you for that.

"But we feel certain that you are brave," she said to him.

He did not feel brave at all. Not now.

"The fourth essential attribute," the Chief Elder said, "is *wisdom*. Jonas has not yet **acquire**d that. The **acquisition** of wisdom will come through his training.

"We are **convince**d that Jonas has the ability to acquire wisdom. That is what we looked for.

"Finally, The Receiver must have one more quality, and it is one which I can only name, but not describe. I do not understand it. You members of the community will not understand it, either. Perhaps Jonas will, because the current Receiver has told us that Jonas already has this quality. He calls it the **Capacity** to See Beyond."

The Chief Elder looked at Jonas with a question in her eyes. The audience watched him, too. They were silent.

For a moment he **froze**, **consume**d with despair. He *didn't* have it, the whatever-she-had-said. He didn't know what it was. Now was the moment when he would have to **confess**, to say, "No, I don't. I *can't*," and throw himself on their **mercy**, ask their forgiveness, to explain that he had been wrongly chosen, that he was not the right one at all.

But when he looked out across the crowd, the sea of faces, the thing happened again. The thing that had happened with the apple.

They *changed.*

He blinked, and it was gone. His shoulders **straightened** slightly. Briefly he felt a tiny **sliver** of sureness for the first time.

She was still watching him. They all were.

"I think it's true," he told the Chief Elder and the community. "I don't understand it yet. I don't know what it is. But sometimes I see something. And maybe it's beyond."

She took her arm from his shoulders.

"Jonas," she said, speaking not to him alone but to the entire community of which he was a part, "you will be trained to be our next Receiver of Memory. We thank you for your childhood."

Then she turned and left the stage, left him there alone, standing and facing the crowd, which began **spontaneously** the collective murmur of his name.

"Jonas." It was a whisper at first: **hushed**, **barely audible**. "Jonas. Jonas."

Then louder, faster. "JONAS. JONAS. JONAS."

With the **chant**, Jonas knew, the community was accepting him and his new role, giving him life, the way they had given it to the newchild Caleb. His heart **swell**ed with **gratitude** and pride.

But at the same time he was filled with fear. He did not know what his selection meant. He did not know what he was to become.

Or what would become of him.*

---

* what would become of him : 어떤 일이 그에게 일어날지. 'become of…' 는 주로 의문사 what 이나 whatever를 주어로 해서 '…은 어떻게 될까?' 라고 표현할 때 쓰인다. 예를 들어 같은 문장을 과거형 형태로, 'what has become of him?' 이라고 하면 '어떤 일이 그에게 일어났을까? 그는 어떻게 되었을까?' 라는 의미가 된다.

9

Now, for the first time in his twelve years of life, Jonas felt separate, different. He remembered what the Chief **Elder** had said: that his training would be alone and apart.

But his training had not yet begun and already, upon leaving the **Auditorium**, he felt the apartness. Holding the folder she had given him, he made his way through the **throng**, looking for his family unit and for Asher. People moved aside for him. They watched him. He thought he could hear whispers.

"Ash!" he called, **spot**ting his friend near the rows of bicycles. "Ride back with me?"

"Sure." Asher smiled, his usual smile, friendly and familiar. But Jonas felt a moment of **hesitation** from his friend, an uncertainty.

"Congratulations," Asher said.

"You too," Jonas replied. "It was really funny, when she told about the **smacks**. You got more **applause** than almost anybody else."

The other new Twelves **cluster**ed nearby, placing their folders carefully into the carrying containers on the backs of the bikes. In each **dwelling** tonight they would be studying the instructions for the beginning of their training. Each night for years the children had **memorize**d the required lessons for school, often **yawn**ing with **boredom**. Tonight they would all begin eagerly to memorize the rules for their adult Assignments.

"Congratulations, Asher!" someone called. Then that hesitation again. "You too, Jonas!"

Asher and Jonas responded with congratulations to their groupmates. Jonas saw his parents watching him from the place where their own bicycles were waiting. Lily had already been **strap**ped into her seat.

He waved. They waved back, smiling, but he noticed that Lily was watching him **solemn**ly, her thumb in her mouth.

He rode directly to his dwelling, exchanging only small jokes and unimportant **remark**s with Asher.

"See you in the morning, Recreation Director!" he called, **dismount**ing by his door as Asher continued on.

"Right! See you!" Asher called back. Once again, there

was just a moment when things weren't quite the same, weren't quite as they had always been through the long friendship. Perhaps he had imagined it. Things couldn't change, with Asher.

The evening meal was quieter than usual. Lily **chattere**d about her plans for **volunteer** work; she would begin, she said, at the Nurturing Center, since she was already an **expert** at feeding Gabriel.

"I know," she added quickly, when her father gave her a warning glance, "I won't mention his name. I know I'm not supposed to know his name.

"I can't wait for tomorrow to come," she said happily.

Jonas sighed uneasily. "I can," he **mutter**ed.

"You've been greatly honored," his mother said. "Your father and I are very proud."

"It's the most important job in the community," Father said.

"But just the other night, you said that the job of making **Assign**ments was the most important!"

Mother nodded. "This is different. It's not a *job*, really. I never thought, never expected—" She paused. "There's only one Receiver."

"But the Chief Elder said that they had made a selection before, and that it failed. What was she talking about?"

Both of his parents **hesitated**. Finally his father described the previous selection. "It was very much as it was today, Jonas—the same **suspense**, as one Eleven had been passed over when the Assignments were given. Then the announcement, when they **singled out** the one—"

Jonas interrupted. "What was his name?"

His mother replied, "Her, not his. It was a female. But we are never to speak the name, or to use it again for a newchild."

Jonas was shocked. A name designated Not-to-Be-Spoken **indicate**d the highest degree of **disgrace**.

"What happened to her?" he asked nervously.

But his parents looked **blank**. "We don't know," his father said uncomfortably. "We never saw her again."

A silence fell over the room. They looked at each other. Finally his mother, rising from the table, said, "You've been greatly honored, Jonas. Greatly honored."

Alone in his sleepingroom, prepared for bed, Jonas opened his folder at last. Some of the other Twelves, he had noticed, had been given folders thick with printed pages. He imagined Benjamin, the scientific male in his group, beginning to read pages of rules and instructions with **relish**. He pictured Fiona smiling her gentle smile as she bent over the lists of duties and methods that she would be required to learn in the days to come.

But his own folder was startlingly close to empty. Inside there was only a single printed sheet. He read it twice.

JONAS

RECEIVER OF MEMORY

1. Go immediately at the end of school hours each day to the **Annex** entrance behind the House of the Old and present yourself to the attendant.

2. Go immediately to your dwelling at the conclusion of Training Hours each day.

3. From this moment you are **exempt**ed from rules **govern**ing rudeness. You may ask any question of any citizen and you will receive answers.

4. Do not discuss your training with any other member of the community, including parents and Elders.

5. From this moment you are **prohibit**ed from dream-telling.

6. Except for illness or **injury** unrelated to your training, do not apply for any **medication**.

7. You are not **permit**ted to apply for **release**.

8. You may lie.

Jonas was **stun**ned. What would happen to his friendships? His mindless hours playing ball, or riding his bike along the river? Those had been happy and **vital** times for him. Were they to be completely taken from him, now? The simple **logistic** instructions—where to go, and when—were expected. Every Twelve had to be told, of course, where and how and when to report for training. But he was a little **dismay**ed that his schedule left no time, **apparent**ly, for recreation.

The exemption from rudeness startled him. Reading it again, however, he realized that it didn't **compel** him to be rude; it simply allowed him the option. He was quite certain he would never take advantage of it. He was so completely, so **thorough**ly **accustom**ed to **courtesy** within the community that the thought of asking another citizen an **intimate** question, of calling someone's attention to an area of **awkward**ness, was **unnerving**.

The **prohibition** of dream-telling, he thought, would not be a real problem. He dreamed so rarely that the dream-telling did not come easily to him anyway, and he was glad to be excused from it. He wondered briefly, though, how to deal with it at the morning meal. What if he *did* dream—should he simply tell his family unit, as he did so often, anyway, that he hadn't? That would be a lie. Still, the final rule said . . . well, he wasn't quite ready to think about the final rule on the page.

The **restriction** of medication unnerved him. Medication was always available to citizens, even to children, through their parents. When he had **crush**ed his finger in the door, he had quickly, **gasp**ing into the speaker, **notified** his mother; she had **hastily requisition**ed relief-of-pain medication which had **prompt**ly been delivered to his dwelling. Almost instantly the **excruciating** pain in his hand had **diminish**ed to the **throb** which was, now, all he could recall of the experience.

Re-reading rule number 6, he realized that a crushed finger fell into the category of "unrelated to training." So if it ever happened again—and he was quite certain it wouldn't; he had been very careful near heavy doors since the accident!—he could still receive medication.

The **pill** he took now, each morning, was also unrelated to training. So he would continue to receive the pill.

But he remembered uneasily what the Chief Elder had said about the pain that would come with his training. She had called it **indescribable**.

Jonas **swallow**ed hard, trying without success to imagine

what such pain might be like, with no medication at all. But it was beyond his comprehension.

He felt no reaction to rule number 7 at all. It had never occurred to him that under any circumstances, ever, he might apply for release.

Finally he **steel**ed himself to read the final rule again. He had been trained since earliest childhood, since his earliest learning of language, never to lie. It was an **integral** part of the learning of **precise** speech. Once, when he had been a Four, he had said, just prior to the midday meal at school, "I'm **starving**."

Immediately he had been taken aside for a brief private lesson in language **precision**. He was not starving, it was pointed out. He was *hungry*. No one in the community was starving, had ever been starving, would ever be starving. To say "starving" was to speak a lie. An **unintentioned** lie, of course. But the reason for precision of language was to **ensure** that unintentional lies were never **utter**ed. Did he understand that? they asked him. And he had.

He had never, within his memory, been **tempt**ed to lie. Asher did not lie. Lily did not lie. His parents did not lie. No one did. Unless . . .

Now Jonas had a thought that he had never had before. This new thought was **frighten**ing. What if *others—adults*—had, upon becoming Twelves, received in *their* instructions the same **terrifying** sentence?

What if they had all been instructed: *You may lie*?

His mind **reeled**. Now, **empowered** to ask questions of **utmost** rudeness—and promised answers—he *could*, **conceivably** (though it was almost unimaginable), ask someone, some adult, his father perhaps: "Do you lie?"

But he would have no way of knowing if the answer he received were true.

10

"I go in here, Jonas," Fiona told him when they reached the front door of the House of the Old after parking their bicycles in the **designate**d area.

"I don't know why I'm nervous," she confessed. "I've been here so often before." She turned her folder over in her hands.

"Well, everything's different now," Jonas reminded her.

"Even the nameplates on our bikes," Fiona laughed. During the night the nameplate of each new Twelve had been removed by the Maintenance Crew and replaced with the style that **indicate**d citizen-in-training.

"I don't want to be late," she said hastily, and started up the steps. "If we finish at the same time, I'll ride home with you."

Jonas nodded, waved to her, and headed around the

building toward the **Annex**, a small wing **attach**ed to the back. He certainly didn't want to be late for his first day of training, either.

The Annex was very **ordinary**, its door un**remarkable**. He reached for the heavy handle, then noticed a **buzzer** on the wall. So he buzzed instead.

"Yes?" The voice came through a small speaker above the buzzer.

"It's, uh, Jonas. I'm the new—I mean—"

"Come in." A **click** indicated that the door had been **unlatch**ed.

The lobby was very small and contained only a desk at which a female **Attendant** sat working on some papers. She looked up when he entered; then, to his surprise, she stood. It was a small thing, the standing; but no one had ever stood automatically to **acknowledge** Jonas's presence before.

"Welcome, Receiver of Memory," she said **respectfully**.

"Oh, please," he replied uncomfortably. "Call me Jonas."

She smiled, pushed a button, and he heard a click that unlocked the door to her left. "You may go right on in," she told him.

Then she seemed to notice his **discomfort** and to realize its origin. No doors in the community were locked, ever. None that Jonas knew of, anyway.

"The locks are simply to **insure** The Receiver's privacy because he needs **concentration**," she explained. "It would be difficult if citizens **wander**ed in, looking for the Department of Bicycle Repair, or something."

Jonas laughed, relaxing a little. The woman seemed very friendly, and it was true—in fact it was a joke throughout the community—that the Department of Bicycle Repair, an unimportant little office, was **relocate**d so often that no one ever knew where it was.

"There is nothing dangerous here," she told him.

"But," she added, **glancing** at the wall clock, "he doesn't like to be kept waiting."

Jonas hurried through the door and found himself in a comfortably **furnish**ed living area. It was not unlike his own family unit's dwelling. Furniture was standard throughout the community: **practical, sturdy**, the function of each piece clearly defined. A bed for sleeping. A table for eating. A desk for studying.

All of those things were in this **spacious** room, though each was slightly different from those in his own dwelling. The **fabrics** on the **upholster**ed chairs and sofa were slightly thicker and more **luxurious**; the table legs were not straight like those at home, but **slender** and curved, with a small **carved decoration** at the foot. The bed, in an **alcove** at the far end of the room, was **drape**d with a **splendid** cloth **embroider**ed over its entire surface with **intricate** designs.

But the most **conspicuous** difference was the books. In his own dwelling, there were the necessary **reference** volumes that each household contained: a dictionary, and the thick community volume which contained descriptions of every office, factory, building, and **committee**. And the Book of Rules, of course.

The books in his own dwelling were the only books that Jonas had ever seen. He had never known that other books existed.

But this room's walls were completely covered by **bookcase**s, filled, which reached to the ceiling. There must have been hundreds—perhaps thousands—of books, their titles **emboss**ed in shiny letters.

Jonas stared at them. He couldn't imagine what the thousands of pages contained. Could there be rules beyond the rules that governed the community? Could there be more descriptions of offices and factories and committees?

He had only a second to look around because he was aware that the man sitting in a chair beside the table was watching him. Hastily he moved forward, stood before the man, **bow**ed slightly, and said, "I'm Jonas."

"I know. Welcome, Receiver of Memory."

Jonas recognized the man. He was the Elder who had

seemed separate from the others at the **Ceremony**, though he was dressed in the same special clothing that only Elders wore.

Jonas looked **self-consciously** into the pale eyes that mirrored his own.

"Sir, I apologize for my lack of understanding . . ."

He waited, but the man did not give the standard accepting-of-apology response.

After a moment, Jonas went on, "But I thought—I mean I *think*," he corrected, reminding himself that if precision of language were ever to be important, it was certainly important *now*, in the presence of this man, "that *you* are the receiver of Memory. I'm only, well, I was only assigned, I mean selected, yesterday. I'm not anything at all. Not yet."

The man looked at him thoughtfully, silently. It was a look that combined interest, **curiosity**, concern, and perhaps a little **sympathy** as well.

Finally he spoke. "Beginning today, this moment, at least to me, you are The Receiver.

"I have been The Receiver for a long time. A very, very long time. You can see that, can't you?"

Jonas nodded. The man was **wrinkled**, and his *eyes*, though **piercing** in their unusual lightness, seemed tired. The **flesh** around them was darkened into shadowed circles.

"I can see that you are very old," Jonas responded with respect. The Old were always given the highest respect.

The man smiled. He touched the **sagging** flesh on his own face with **amuse**ment. "I am not, actually, as old as I look," he told Jonas. "This job has aged me. I know I look as if I should be scheduled for release very soon. But actually I have a good deal of time left.

"I was pleased, though, when you were selected. It took them a long time. The failure of the previous selection was ten years ago, and my energy is starting to **diminish**. I need what strength I have remaining for your training. We have hard and painful work to do, you and I.

"Please sit down," he said, and gestured toward the nearby chair. Jonas lowered himself onto the soft **cushion**ed seat.

The man closed his eyes and continued speaking. "When I became a Twelve, I was selected, as you were. I was frightened, as I'm sure you are." He opened his eyes for a moment and **peer**ed at Jonas, who nodded.

The eyes closed again. "I came to this very room to begin my training. It was such a long time ago.

"The previous Receiver seemed just as old to me as I do to you. He was just as tired as I am today."

He sat forward suddenly, opened his eyes, and said, "You may ask questions. I have so little experience in describing this process. It is **forbidden** to talk of it."

"I know, sir. I have read the instructions," Jonas said.

"So I may **neglect** to make things as clear as I should." The man **chuckled**. "My job is important and has **enormous** honor. But that does not mean I am perfect, and when I tried before to train a **successor**, I failed. Please ask any questions that will help you."

In his mind, Jonas had questions. A thousand. A *million* questions. As many questions as there were books lining the walls. But he did not ask one, not yet.

The man sighed, seeming to put his thoughts in order. Then he spoke again. "Simply stated," he said, "although it's not really simple at all, my job is to **transmit** to you all the memories I have within me. Memories of the past."

"Sir," Jonas said **tentatively**, "I would be very interested to hear the story of your life, and to listen to your memories.

"I apologize for interrupting," he added quickly.

The man waved his hand **impatiently**. "No apologies in this room. We haven't time."

"Well," Jonas went on, uncomfortably aware that he might be interrupting again, "I am really interested, I don't mean that I'm not. But I don't exactly understand why it's so important. I could do some adult job in the community, and in my recreation time I could come and listen to the stories from your childhood. I'd like that. Actually," he added, "I've done that already, in the House of the Old. The Old like to tell about their childhoods, and it's always fun to listen."

The man shook his head. "No, no," he said. "I'm not being clear. It's not my past, not my childhood that I must transmit to you."

He leaned back, resting his head against the back of the upholstered chair. "It's the memories of the whole world," he said with a sigh. "Before you, before me, before the previous Receiver, and generations before him."

Jonas **frowned**. "The whole world?" he asked. "I don't understand. Do you mean not just us? Not just the community? Do you mean Elsewhere, too?" He tried, in his mind, to **grasp** the concept. "I'm sorry, sir. I don't understand exactly. Maybe I'm not smart enough. I don't know what you mean when you say 'the whole world' or 'generations before him.' I thought there was only us. I thought there was only now."

"There's much more. There's all that goes beyond—all that is Elsewhere—and all that goes back, and back, and back. I received all of those, when I was selected. And here in this room, all alone, I re-experience them again and again. It is how wisdom comes. And how we shape our future."

He rested for a moment, breathing deeply. "I am so

weighted with them," he said.

Jonas felt a terrible concern for the man, suddenly.

"It's as if . . ." The man paused, seeming to search his mind for the right words of description. "It's like going downhill through deep snow on a **sled**," he said, finally. "At first it's **exhilarating**: the speed; the sharp, clear air; but then the snow **accumulates**, builds up on the runners, and you slow, you have to push hard to keep going, and—"

He shook his head suddenly, and peered at Jonas. "That meant nothing to you, did it?" he asked.

Jonas was confused. "I didn't understand it, sir."

"Of course you didn't. You don't know what snow is, do you?"

Jonas shook his head.

"Or a sled? Runners?"

"No, sir," Jonas said.

"Downhill? The term means nothing to you?"

"Nothing, sir."

Well, it's a place to start. I'd been wondering how to begin. Move to the bed, and lie face down. Remove your **tunic** first."

Jonas did so, a little **apprehensively**. Beneath his **bare** chest, he felt the soft folds of the **magnificent** cloth that covered the bed. He watched as the man rose and moved first to the wall where the speaker was. It was the same sort of speaker that occupied a place in every dwelling, but one thing about it was different. This one had a switch, which the man **deftly snap**ped to the end that said OFF.

Jonas almost gasped aloud. To have the power to turn the speaker *off*. It was an **astonish**ing thing.

Then the man moved with surprising quickness to the corner where the bed was. He sat on a chair beside Jonas, who was motionless, waiting for what would happen next.

"Close your eyes. Relax. This will not be painful."

Jonas remembered that he was allowed, that he had even been **encourage**d, to ask questions. "What are you going to do, sir?" he asked, hoping that his voice didn't **betray** his nervousness.

"I am going to transmit the memory of snow," the old man said, and placed his hands on Jonas's bare back.

11

Jonas felt nothing unusual at first. He felt only the light touch of the old man's hands on his back.

He tried to relax, to breathe **even**ly. The room was absolutely silent, and for a moment Jonas feared that he might **disgrace** himself now, on the first day of his training, by falling asleep.

Then he **shiver**ed. He realized that the touch of the hands felt, suddenly, cold. At the same instant, breathing in, he felt the air change, and his very breath was cold. He **lick**ed his lips, and in doing so, his tongue touched the suddenly **chill**ed air.

It was very **startling**; but he was not at all frightened, now. He was filled with energy, and he breathed again, feeling the sharp **intake** of **frigid** air. Now, too, he could feel cold air **swirl**ing around his entire body. He felt it blow against his hands where they lay at his sides, and over his back.

The touch of the man's hands seemed to have disappeared.

Now he became aware of an entirely new sensation: **pinpricks**? No, because they were soft and without pain. Tiny, cold, featherlike feelings **pepper**ed his body and face. He put out his tongue again, and caught one of the dots of cold upon it. It disappeared from his awareness instantly; but he caught another, and another. The sensation made him smile.

One part of his consciousness knew that he was still lying there, on the bed, in the Annex room. Yet another, separate part of his being was **upright** now, in a sitting position, and beneath him he could feel that he was not on the soft **decorate**d bedcovering at all, but rather seated on a flat, hard surface. His hands now held (though at the same time they were still motionless at his sides) a rough, **damp** rope.

And he could *see*, though his eyes were closed. He could see a bright, **whirling torrent** of crystals in the air around him, and he could see them gather on the backs of his hands, like cold **fur**.

His breath was visible.

Beyond, through the swirl of what he now, somehow,

perceived was the thing the old man had spoken of—*snow*—he could look out and down a great distance. He was up high someplace. The ground was thick with the **furry** snow, but he sat slightly above it on a hard, flat object.

Sled, he knew **abruptly**. He was sitting on a thing called *sled*. And the sled itself seemed to be **poise**d at the top of a long, **extend**ed **mound** that rose from the very land where he was. Even as he thought the word "mound," his new consciousness told him *hill*.

Then the sled, with Jonas himself upon it, began to move through the snowfall, and he understood instantly that now he was going downhill. No voice made an explanation. The experience explained itself to him.

His face cut through the frigid air as he began the **descent**, moving through the substance called snow on the **vehicle** called sled, which **propel**led itself on what he now knew without doubt to be *runners*.

Comprehending all of those things as he sped downward, he was free to enjoy the **breathless glee** that **overwhelm**ed him: the speed, the clear cold air, the total silence, the feeling of balance and excitement and peace.

Then, as the angle of **incline** lessened, as the mound—the *hill*—flattened, nearing the bottom, the sled's forward motion slowed. The snow was piled now around it, and he pushed with his body, moving it forward, not wanting the **exhilarating** ride to end.

Finally the **obstruction** of the piled snow was too much for the thin runners of the sled, and he came to a stop. He sat there for a moment, **pant**ing, holding the rope in his cold hands. **Tentative**ly he opened his eyes—not his snow-hill-sled eyes, for they had been open throughout the strange ride. He opened his **ordinary** eyes, and saw that he was still on the bed, that he had not moved at all.

The old man, still beside the bed, was watching him. "How do you feel?" he asked.

Jonas sat up and tried to answer honestly. "Surprised," he said, after a moment.

The old man **wiped** his **forehead** with his **sleeve**. "Whew," he said. "It was **exhaust**ing. But you know, even **transmit**ting that tiny memory to you—I think it lightened me just a little."

"Do you mean—you did say I could ask questions:"

The man nodded, **encouraging** his question.

"Do you mean that now you don't have the memory of it—of that ride on the sled—anymore?"

"That's right. A little weight off this old body."

"But it was such fun! And now you don't have it anymore! I *took* it from you!"

But the old man laughed. "All I gave you was one ride,

on one sled, in one snow, on one hill. I have a whole world of them in my memory. I could give them to you one by one, a thousand times, and there would still be more."

"Are you saying that I—I mean we—could do it again?" Jonas asked. "I'd really like to. I think I could **steer**, by pulling the rope. I didn't try this time, because it was so new."

The old man, laughing, shook his head. "Maybe another day, for a **treat**. But there's no time, really, just to play. I only wanted to begin by showing you how it works.

"Now," he said, turning **businesslike**, "Lie back down. I want to—"

Jonas did. He was **eager** for whatever experience would come next. But he had, suddenly, so many questions.

"Why don't we have snow, and sleds, and hills?" he asked. "And when did we, in the past? Did my parents have sleds when they were young? Did you?"

The old man **shrugged** and gave a short laugh. "No," he told Jonas. "It's a very distant memory. That's why it was so exhausting—I had to **tug** it forward from many generations back. It was given to me when I was a new Receiver, and the previous Receiver had to pull it through a long time period, too."

"But what happened to those things? Snow, and the rest of it?"

"Climate Control. Snow made growing food difficult, limited the **agricultural** periods. And un**predictable** weather made transportation almost impossible at times. It wasn't a **practical** thing, so it became **obsolete** when we went to Sameness.

"And hills, too," he added. "They made **conveyance** of goods **unwieldy**. Trucks; buses. Slowed them down. So—" He waved his hand, as if a gesture had caused hills to disappear. "Sameness," he concluded.

Jonas frowned. "I wish we had those things, still. Just **now and then**."

The old man smiled. "So do I" he said. "But that choice is not ours."

"But sir," Jonas suggested, "since you have so much power—"

The man corrected him. "Honor," he said firmly. "I have great honor. So will you. But you will find that that is not the same as power.

"Lie quietly now. Since we've entered into the topic of climate, let me give you something else. And this time I'm not going to tell you the name of it, because I want to test the receiving. You should be able to perceive the name without being told. I gave away snow and sled and downhill and runners by telling them to you in advance."

Without being instructed, Jonas closed his eyes again.

He felt the hands on his back again. He waited.

Now it came more quickly, the feelings. This time the hands didn't become cold, but instead began to feel warm on his body. They **moisten**ed a little. The warmth spread, extending across his shoulders, up his neck, onto the side of his face. He could feel it through his clothed parts, too: a pleasant, all-over sensation; and when he licked his lips this time, the air was hot and heavy.

He didn't move. There was no sled. His **posture** didn't change. He was simply alone someplace, out of doors, lying down, and the warmth came from far above. It was not as exciting as the ride through the snowy air; but it was **pleasurable** and comforting.

Suddenly he perceived the word for it: *sunshine.* He perceived that it came from the sky.

Then it ended.

"Sunshine," he said aloud, opening his eyes.

"Good. You did get the word. That makes my job easier. Not so much explaining."

"And it came from the sky."

"That's right," the old man said. "Just the way it used to."

"Before Sameness. Before Climate Control," Jonas added.

The man laughed. "You receive well, and learn quickly.

I'm very pleased with you. That's enough for today, I think. We're off to a good start."

There was a question bothering Jonas. "Sir," he said, "The Chief Elder told me—she told everyone—and you told me, too, that it would be painful. So I was a little scared. But it didn't hurt at all. I really enjoyed it." He looked **quizzically** at the old man.

The man sighed. "I started you with memories of pleasure. My previous failure gave me the wisdom to do that." He took a few deep breaths. "Jonas," he said, "it *will* be painful. But it need not be painful yet."

"I'm brave. I really am." Jonas sat up a little straighter.

The old man looked at him for a moment. He smiled. "I can see that," he said. "Well, since you asked the question—I think I have enough energy for one more **transmission**.

"Lie down once more. This will be the last today."

Jonas **obeyed** cheerfully. He closed his eyes, waiting, and felt the hands again; then he felt the warmth again, the sunshine again, coming from the sky of this other consciousness that was so new to him. This time, as he lay **basking** in the wonderful warmth, he felt the passage of time. His real self was aware that it was only a minute or two; but his other, memory-receiving self felt hours pass in the sun. His skin began to **sting**. **Restlessly** he moved one arm, bending it, and felt a sharp pain in the **crease** of his inner arm at the elbow.

"Ouch," he said loudly, and **shift**ed on the bed. "Owww," he said, **wincing** at the shift, and even moving his mouth to speak made his face hurt.

He knew there was a word, but the pain kept him from grasping it.

Then it ended. He opened his eyes, wincing with discomfort. "It hurt," he told the man, "and I couldn't get the word for it."

"It was **sunburn**," the old man told him.

"It hurt a *lot*," Jonas said, "but I'm glad you gave it to me. It was interesting. And now I understand better, what it meant, that there would be pain."

The man didn't respond. He sat silently for a second. Finally he said, "Get up, now. It's time for you to go home."

They both walked to the center of the room. Jonas put his tunic back on. "Goodbye, sir," he said. "Thank you for my first day."

The old man nodded to him. He looked **drain**ed, and a little sad.

"Sir?" Jonas said shyly.

"Yes? Do you have a question?"

"It's just that I don't know your name. I thought you were The Receiver, but you say that now *I'm* The Receiver.

So I don't know what to call you."

The man had sat back down in the comfortable **upholstered** chair. He moved his shoulders around as if to ease away an aching sensation. He seemed terribly **weary**.

"Call me The Giver," he told Jonas.

12

"You **slept soundly**, Jonas?" his mother asked at the morning meal. "No dreams?"

Jonas simply smiled and nodded, not ready to lie, not willing to tell the truth. "I slept very soundly," he said.

"I wish this one would," his father said, leaning down from his chair to touch Gabriel's waving **fist**. The basket was on the floor beside him; in its corner, beside Gabriel's head, the stuffed **hippo** sat staring with its **blank** eyes.

"So do I," Mother said, rolling her eyes. "He's so **fretful** at night."

Jonas had not heard the newchild during the night because as always, he *had* slept soundly. But it was not true that he had no dreams.

Again and again, as he slept, he had slid down that snow-covered hill. Always, in the dream, it seemed as if there were a **destination**: a *something*—he could not grasp what—that lay beyond the place where the thickness of snow brought the sled to a stop.

He was left, upon awakening, with the feeling that he wanted, even somehow needed, to reach the something that waited in the distance. The feeling that it was good. That it was welcoming. That it was **significant**.

But he did not know how to get there.

He tried to **shed** the **leftover** dream, gathering his schoolwork and preparing for the day.

School seemed a little different today. The classes were the same: language and communications; **commerce** and industry; science and technology; civil **procedure**s and **govern**ment. But during the breaks for recreation periods and the midday meal, the other new Twelves were **abuzz** with descriptions of their first day of training. All of them talked at once, interrupting each other, **hastily** making the required **apology** for interrupting, then forgetting again in the excitement of describing the new experiences.

Jonas listened. He was very aware of his own **admonition** not to discuss his training. But it would have been impossible, anyway. There was no way to describe to his friends what he had experienced there in the Annex room. How could you describe a sled without describing a hill and snow; and how could you describe a hill and snow to someone who had never felt height or wind or that **feathery**, magical cold?

Even trained for years as they all had been in **precision** of language, what words could you use which would give another the experience of sunshine?

So it was easy for Jonas to be still and to listen.

After school hours he rode again beside Fiona to the House of the Old.

"I looked for you yesterday," she told him, "so we could ride home together. Your bike was still there, and I waited for a little while. But it was getting late, so I went on home."

"I apologize for making you wait," Jonas said.

"I accept your apology," she replied automatically.

"I stayed a little longer than I expected," Jonas explained.

She **pedal**ed forward silently, and he knew that she expected him to tell her why. She expected him to describe his first day of training. But to ask would have fallen into the category of rudeness.

"You've been doing so many **volunteer** hours with the Old," Jonas said, changing the subject. "There won't be much that you don't already know."

"Oh, there's lots to learn," Fiona replied. "There's **administrative** work, and the **dietary** rules, and **punish**ment for **disobedience**—did you know that they use a

discipline wand on the Old, the same as for small children? And there's **occupational therapy**, and recreational activities, and **medications**, and—"

They reached the building and braked their bikes.

"I really think I'll like it better than school," Fiona **confessed**.

"Me too," Jonas agreed, wheeling his bike into its place.

She waited for a second, as if, again, she expected him to go on. Then she looked at her watch, waved, and hurried toward the entrance.

Jonas stood for a moment beside his bike, startled. It had happened again: the thing that he thought of now as "seeing beyond." This time it had been Fiona who had undergone that **fleeting indescribable** change. As he looked up and toward her going through the door, it happened; she changed. Actually, Jonas thought, trying to recreate it in his mind, it wasn't Fiona in her **entirety**. It seemed to be just her hair. And just for that **flicker**ing instant.

He ran through it in his mind. It was clearly beginning to happen more often. First, the apple a few weeks before. The next time had been the faces in the audience at the **Auditorium**, just two days ago. Now, today, Fiona's hair.

Frowning, Jonas walked toward the Annex. I will ask The Giver, he decided.

The old man looked up, smiling, when Jonas entered

the room. He was already seated beside the bed, and he seemed more **energetic** today, slightly renewed, and glad to see Jonas.

"Welcome," he said. "We must get started. You're one minute late."

"I apologi—" Jonas began, and then stopped, **flustered**, remembering there were to be no apologies.

He removed his tunic and went to the bed. "I'm one minute late because something happened," he explained. "And I'd like to ask you about it, if you don't mind."

"You may ask me anything."

Jonas tried to sort it out in his mind so that he could explain it clearly. "I think it's what you call seeing-beyond," he said.

The Giver nodded. "Describe it," he said.

Jonas told him about the experience with the apple. Then the moment on the stage, when he had looked out and seen the same **phenomenon** in the faces of the crowd.

"Then today, just now, outside, it happened with my friend Fiona. She herself didn't change, exactly. But something about her changed for a second. Her hair looked different; but not in its shape, not in its length. I can't quite—" Jonas paused, **frustrated** by his inability to grasp and describe exactly what *had* occurred.

Finally he simply said, "It changed. I don't know how,

or why.

"That's why I was one minute late," he concluded, and looked **questioning**ly at The Giver.

To his surprise, the old man asked him a question which seemed unrelated to the seeing-beyond. "When I gave you the memory yesterday, the first one, the ride on the sled, did you look around?"

Jonas nodded. "Yes," he said, "but the stuff—I mean the snow—in the air made it hard to see anything."

"Did you look at the sled?"

Jonas thought back. "No. I only felt it under me. I dreamed of it last night, too. But I don't remember *seeing* the sled in my dream, either. Just feeling it."

The Giver seemed to be thinking.

"When I was **observing** you, before the selection, I **perceived** that you probably had the **capacity**, and what you describe confirms that. It happened somewhat differently to me," The Giver told him. "When I was just your age—about to become the new Receiver—I began to experience it, though it took a different form. With me it was . . . well, I won't describe that now; you wouldn't understand it yet.

"But I think I can guess how it's happening with you. Let me just make a little test, to confirm my guess. Lie down."

Jonas lay on the bed again with his hands at his sides.

He felt comfortable here now. He closed his eyes and waited for the familiar feel of The Giver's hands on his back.

But it didn't come. Instead, The Giver instructed him, "Call back the memory of the ride on the sled. Just the *beginning* of it, where you're at the top of the hill, before the slide starts. And this time, look down at the sled."

Jonas was **puzzled**. He opened his eyes. "Excuse me," he asked politely, "but don't *you* have to give me the memory?"

"It's your memory, now, It's not mine to experience any longer. I gave it away."

"But how can I call it back?"

"You can remember last year, or the year that you were a Seven, or a Five, can't you?"

"Of course."

"It's much the same. Everyone in the community has one-generation memories like those. But now you will be able to go back farther. Try. Just **concentrate**."

Jonas closed his eyes again. He took a deep breath and **sought** the sled and the hill and the snow in his consciousness.

There they were, with no effort. He was again sitting in that **whirl**ing world of **snowflake**s, atop the hill.

Jonas **grin**ned with delight, and blew his own steamy breath into view. Then, as he had been instructed, he looked down. He saw his own hands, **fur**red again with snow, holding the rope. He saw his legs, and moved them aside for a **glimpse** of the sled beneath.

Dumbfounded, he stared at it. This time it was not a fleeting **impression**. This time the sled had—and continued to have, as he **blinked**, and stared at it again—that same mysterious quality that the apple had had so briefly. And Fiona's hair. The sled did not change. It simply was—whatever the thing was.

Jonas opened his eyes and was still on the bed. The Giver was watching him curiously.

"Yes," Jonas said slowly. "I saw it, in the sled."

"Let me try one more thing. Look over there, to the **bookcase**. Do you see the very top row of books, the ones behind the table, on the top **shelf**?"

Jonas sought them with his eyes. He stared at them, and they changed. But the change was fleeting. It **slipped** away the next instant.

"It happened," Jonas said. "It happened to the books, but it went away again."

"I'm right, then," The Giver said. "You're beginning to see the color red."

"The what?"

The Giver sighed. "How to explain this? Once, back in the time of the memories, everything had a shape and size, the way things still do, but they also had a quality called *color.*

"There were a lot of colors, and one of them was called red. That's the one you are starting to see. Your friend Fiona has red hair—quite **distinctive**, actually; I've noticed it before. When you mentioned Fiona's hair, it was the **clue** that told me you were probably beginning to see the color red."

"And the faces of people? The ones I saw at the Ceremony?"

The Giver shook his head. "No, **flesh** isn't red. But it has red tones in it. There was a time, actually—you'll see this in the memories later—when flesh was many different colors. That was before we went to Sameness. Today flesh is all the same, and what you saw was the red tones. Probably when you saw the faces take on color it wasn't as deep or **vibrant** as the apple, or your friend's hair."

The Giver **chuckled**, suddenly. "We've never completely mastered Sameness. I suppose the **genetic** scientists are still hard at work trying to **work** the **kinks out.** Hair like Fiona's must **drive them crazy.**"

Jonas listened, trying hard to **comprehend**. "And the sled?" he said. "It had that same thing: the color red. But it didn't *change*, Giver. It just *was.*"

"Because it's a memory from the time when color *was.*"

"It was so—oh, I wish language were more **precise**! The

red was so beautiful!"

The Giver nodded. "It is."

"Do you see it all the time?"

"I see all of them. All the colors."

"Will I?"

"Of course. When you receive the memories. You have the capacity to see beyond. You'll gain wisdom, then, along with colors. And lots more."

Jonas wasn't interested, just then, in wisdom. It was the colors that **fascinate**d him. "Why can't everyone see them? Why did colors disappear?"

The Giver shrugged. "Our people made that choice, the choice to go to Sameness. Before my time, before the previous time, back and back and back. We **relinquish**ed color when we relinquished sunshine and did away with differences." He thought for a moment. "We gained control of many things. But we had to let go of others."

"We shouldn't have!" Jonas said **fierce**ly.

The Giver looked startled at the certainty of Jonas's reaction. Then he smiled **wryly**. "You've come very quickly to that conclusion," he said. "It took me many years. Maybe your wisdom will come much more quickly than mine."

He glanced at the wall clock. "Lie back down, now. We have so much to do."

"Giver," Jonas asked as he arranged himself again on the

bed, "how did it happen to you when you were becoming The Receiver? You said that the seeing-beyond happened to you, but not the same way."

The hands came to his back. "Another day," The Giver said gently. "I'll tell you another day. Now we must work. And I've thought of a way to help you with the concept of color.

"Close your eyes and be still, now. I'm going to give you a memory of a rainbow."

13

Days went by, and weeks. Jonas learned, through the memories, the names of colors; and now he began to see them all, in his ordinary life (though he knew it was ordinary no longer, and would never be again). But they didn't last. There would be a glimpse of green—the landscaped **lawn** around the Central Plaza; a bush on the **riverbank**. The bright orange of pumpkins being **truck**ed in from the **agricultural** fields beyond the community **boundary**—seen in an instant, the **flash** of **brilliant** color, but gone again, returning to their flat and **hueless** shade.

The Giver told him that it would be a very long time before he had the colors to keep.

"But I want them!" Jonas said angrily. "It isn't fair that nothing has color!"

"Not fair?" The Giver looked at Jonas curiously. "Explain

what you mean."

"Well . . ." Jonas had to stop and think it through. "If everything's the same, then there aren't any choices! I want to wake up in the morning and *decide* things! A blue **tunic**, or a red one?"

He looked down at himself, at the colorless **fabric** of his clothing. "But it's all the same, always."

Then he laughed a little. "I know it's not important, what you wear. It doesn't matter. But—"

"It's the choosing that's important, isn't it?" The Giver asked him.

Jonas nodded. "My little brother—" he began, and then corrected himself. "No, that's **inaccurate**. He's not my brother, not really. But this newchild that my family takes care of—his name's Gabriel?"

"Yes, I know about Gabriel."

"Well, he's right at the age where he's learning so much. He grabs toys when we hold them in front of him—my father says he's learning small-**muscle** control. And he's really cute."

The Giver nodded.

"But now that I can see colors, at least sometimes, I was just thinking: what if we could hold up things that were bright red, or bright yellow, and he could *choose*? Instead of the Sameness."

"He might make wrong choices."

"Oh." Jonas was silent for a minute. "Oh, I see what you mean. It wouldn't matter for a newchild's toy. But later it *does* matter, doesn't it? We don't dare to let people make choices of their own."

"Not safe?" The Giver suggested.

"**Definite**ly not safe," Jonas said with certainty. "What if they were allowed to choose their own mate? And chose *wrong*?

"Or what if," he went on, almost laughing at the **absurd**ity, "they chose their own *jobs*?"

"**Frighten**ing, isn't it?" The Giver said.

Jonas **chuckle**d. "Very frightening. I can't even imagine it. We really have to protect people from wrong choices."

"It's safer."

"Yes," Jonas agreed. "Much safer."

But when the conversation turned to other things, Jonas was left, still, with a feeling of **frustration** that he didn't understand.

He found that he was often angry, now: **irrationall**y angry at his groupmates, that they were satisfied with their lives which had none of the **vibrance** his own was taking on. And he was angry at himself, that he could not change that for them.

He tried. Without asking permission from The Giver,

because he feared—or knew—that it would be denied, he tried to give his new awareness to his friends.

"Asher," Jonas said one morning, "look at those flowers very carefully." They were standing beside a bed of geraniums* planted near the Hall of Open Records. He put his hands on Asher's shoulders, and **concentrate**d on the red of the **petal**s, trying to hold it as long as he could, and trying at the same time to transmit the awareness of red to his friend.

"What's the matter?" Asher asked uneasily. "Is something wrong?" He moved away from Jonas's hands. It was extremely rude for one citizen to touch another outside of family units.

"No, nothing. I thought for a minute that they were **wilt**ing, and we should let the Gardening Crew know they needed more watering." Jonas sighed, and turned away.

One evening he came home from his training **weighted** with new knowledge. The Giver had chosen a startling and **disturb**ing memory that day. Under the touch of his hands, Jonas had found himself suddenly in a place that was completely **alien**: hot and windswept under a vast blue sky. There were **tufts** of **sparse** grass, a few bushes and

---

* a bed of geraniums : 제라늄(geranium)꽃의 화단(bed). 제라늄은 다양하고 화려한 색을 가지고 있어 관상용으로 많이 심는 꽃이다. 'bed'가 '침대'가 아닌 '화단, 모판'이라는 의미로 사용된 것에 유의.

rocks, and nearby he could see an area of thicker **vegetation**: broad, low trees outlined against the sky. He could hear noises: the sharp crack of weapons—he perceived the word *guns*—and then shouts, and an **immense** crashing **thud** as something fell, tearing branches from the trees.

He heard voices calling to one another. **Peer**ing from the place where he stood hidden behind some **shrubbery**, he was reminded of what The Giver had told him, that there had been a time when flesh had different colors. Two of these men had dark brown skin; the others were light. Going closer, he watched them **hack** the **tusk**s from a motionless elephant on the ground and **haul** them away, **spatter**ed with blood. He felt himself **overwhelm**ed with a new perception of the color he knew as red.

Then the men were gone, speeding toward the **horizon** in a vehicle that **spit** **pebble**s from its **whirl**ing tires. One hit his **forehead** and **stung** him there. But the memory continued, though Jonas ached now for it to end.

Now he saw another elephant **emerge** from the place where it had stood hidden in the trees. Very slowly it walked to the **mutilate**d body and looked down. With its **sinuous trunk** it **stroke**d the huge **corpse**; then it reached up, broke some **leafy** branches with a **snap**, and **draped** them over the mass of torn thick flesh.

Finally it **tilt**ed its massive head, raised its trunk, and

roared into the empty landscape. Jonas had never heard such a sound. It was a sound of **rage** and **grief** and it seemed never to end.

He could still hear it when he opened his eyes and lay **anguish**ed on the bed where he received the memories. It continued to roar into his consciousness as he **pedal**ed slowly home.

"Lily," he asked that evening when his sister took her comfort object, the stuffed elephant, from the **shelf**, "did you know that once there really were elephants? Live ones?"

She **glance**d down at the **ragged** comfort object and grinned. "Right," she said, **skeptical**ly. "Sure, Jonas."

Jonas went and sat beside them while his father untied Lily's hair ribbons and **comb**ed her hair. He placed one hand on each of their shoulders. With all of his being he tried to give each of them a piece of the memory: not of the **torture**d cry of the elephant, but of the *being* of the elephant, of the **tower**ing, immense creature and the **meticulous** touch with which it had **tend**ed its friend at the end.

But his father had continued to comb Lily's long hair, and Lily, **impatient**, had finally **wiggle**d under her brother's touch. "Jonas," she said, "you're *hurting* me with your hand."

"I **apologize** for hurting you, Lily," Jonas **mumble**d, and took his hand away.

" 'Ccept your apology," Lily responded **indifferent**ly, stroking the lifeless elephant.

"Giver," Jonas asked once, as they prepared for the day's work, "don't you have a **spouse**? Aren't you allowed to apply for one?" Although he was **exempt**ed from the rules against rudeness, he was aware that this was a rude question. But The Giver had **encourage**d all of his questions, not seeming to be **embarrass**ed or **offend**ed by even the most personal.

The Giver chuckled. "No, there's no rule against it. And I did have a spouse. You're forgetting how old I am, Jonas. My former spouse lives now with the Childless Adults."

"Oh, of course." Jonas *had* forgotten The Giver's obvious age. When adults of the community became older, their lives became different. They were no longer needed to create family units. Jonas's own parents, when he and Lily were grown, would go to live with the Childless Adults.

"You'll be able to apply for a spouse, Jonas, if you want to. I'll warn you, though, that it will be difficult. Your living arrangements will have to be different from those of most family units, because the books are **forbidden** to citizens. You and I are the only ones with access to the books."

Jonas glanced around at the **astonish**ing **array** of volumes.

From time to time, now, he could see their colors. With their hours together, his and The Giver's, **consume**d by conversation and by the **transmission** of memories, Jonas had not yet opened any of the books. But he read the titles here and there, and knew that they contained all of the knowledge of centuries, and that one day they would **belong** to him.

"So if I have a spouse, and maybe children, I will have to hide the books from them?"

The Giver nodded. "I wasn't **permit**ted to share the books with my spouse, that's correct. And there are other difficulties, too. You remember the rule that says the new Receiver can't talk about his training?"

Jonas nodded. Of course he remembered. It had turned out, by far, to be the most **frustrating** of the rules he was required to **obey**.

"When you become the official Receiver, when we're finished here, you'll be given a whole new set of rules. Those are the rules that I obey. And it won't surprise you that I am forbidden to talk about my work to anyone except the new Receiver. That's you, of course.

"So there will be a whole part of your life which you won't be able to share with a family. It's hard, Jonas. It was hard for me.

"You do understand, don't you, that this is my life? The

memories?"

Jonas nodded again, but he was puzzled. Didn't life consist of the things you did each day? There wasn't anything else, really. "I've seen you taking walks," he said.

The Giver sighed. "I walk. I eat at mealtime. And when I am called by the **Committee** of **Elders**, I appear before them, to give them **counsel** and advice."

"Do you advise them often?" Jonas was a little frightened at the thought that one day he would be the one to advise the ruling body.

But The Giver said no. "**Rarely**. Only when they are faced with something that they have not experienced before. Then they call upon me to use the memories and advise them. But it very **seldom** happens. Sometimes I wish they'd ask for my wisdom more often—there are so many things I could tell them; things I wish they would change. But they don't want change. Life here is so orderly, so **predictable**—so painless. It's what they've chosen."

"I don't know why they even *need* a Receiver, then, if they never call upon him," Jonas commented.

"They need me. And you," The Giver said, but didn't explain. "They were reminded of that ten years ago."

"What happened ten years ago?" Jonas asked. "Oh, I know. You tried to train a **successor** and it failed. Why? Why did that remind them?"

The Giver smiled **grimly**. "When the new Receiver failed, the memories that she had received were **released**. They didn't come back to me. They went . . ."

He paused, and seemed to be **struggling** with the concept. "I don't know, exactly. They went to the place where memories once existed before Receivers were created. Someplace out *there*—" He gestured **vaguely** with his arm. "And then the people had access to them. **Apparently** that's the way it was, once. Everyone had access to memories.

"It was chaos," he said. "They really suffered for a while. Finally it **subsided** as the memories were **assimilated**. But it certainly made them aware of how they need a Receiver to contain all that pain. And knowledge."

"But you have to suffer like that all the time," Jonas pointed out.

The Giver nodded. "And you will. It's my life. It will be yours."

Jonas thought about it, about what it would be like for him. "Along with walking and eating and—" He looked around the walls of books. "Reading? That's it?"

The Giver shook his head. "Those are simply the things that I *do*, My *life* is here."

"In this room?"

The Giver shook his head. He put his hands to his own face, to his **chest**. "No. Here, in my being. Where the memories are."

"My Instructors in science and technology have taught us about how the brain works," Jonas told him eagerly. "It's full of **electrical impulses**. It's like a computer. If you **stimulate** one part of the brain with an **electrode**, it—" He stopped talking. He could see an odd look on The Giver's face.

"They know nothing," The Giver said **bitter**ly.

Jonas was shocked. Since the first day in the **Annex** room, they had together **disregard**ed the rules about rudeness, and Jonas felt comfortable with that now. But this was different, and far beyond rude. This was a terrible **accusation**. What if someone had heard?

He glanced quickly at the wall speaker, **terrified** that the Committee might be listening as they could at any time. But, as always during their **session**s together, the switch had been turned to OFF.

"Nothing?" Jonas whispered nervously. "But my instructors—"

The Giver **flick**ed his hand as if brushing something aside. "Oh, your instructors are well trained. They know their scientific facts. *Everyone* is well trained for his job.

"It's just that . . . without the memories it's all meaningless. They gave that **burden** to me. And to the previous Receiver. And the one before him."

"And back and back and back," Jonas said, knowing the **phrase** that always came.

The Giver smiled, though his smile was oddly **harsh**. "That's right. And next it will be you. A great honor."

"Yes, sir. They told me that at the **Ceremony**. The very highest honor."

Some afternoons The Giver sent him away without training. Jonas knew, on days when he arrived to find The Giver **hunch**ed over, rocking his body slightly back and forth, his face pale, that he would be sent away.

"Go," The Giver would tell him **tense**ly. "I'm in pain today. Come back tomorrow."

On those days, worried and disappointed, Jonas would walk alone beside the river. The paths were empty of people except for the few Delivery Crews and Landscape Workers here and there. Small children were all at the Childcare Center after school, and the older ones busy with volunteer hours or training.

By himself, he tested his own developing memory. He watched the landscape for glimpses of the green that he knew was **embed**ded in the shrubbery; when it came **flick-ering** into his consciousness, he focused upon it, keeping it there, darkening it, holding it in his vision as long as possible until his head hurt and he let it fade away.

He stared at the flat, colorless sky, bringing blue from it, and remembered sunshine until finally, for an instant, he could feel warmth.

He stood at the foot of the bridge that **span**ned the river, the bridge that citizens were allowed to cross only on official business. Jonas had crossed it on school trips, visiting the **outlying** communities, and he knew that the land beyond the bridge was much the same, flat and well ordered, with fields for **agriculture**. The other communities he had seen on visits were essentially the same as his own, the only differences were slightly **alter**ed styles of **dwelling**s, slightly different schedules in the schools.

He wondered what lay in the far distance where he had never gone. The land didn't *end* beyond those nearby communities. Were there *hills* Elsewhere? Were there vast wind-torn areas like the place he had seen in memory, the place where the elephant died?

"Giver," he asked one afternoon following a day when he had been sent away, "what causes you pain?"

When The Giver was silent, Jonas continued. "The Chief Elder told me, at the beginning, that the receiving of memory causes terrible pain. And you described for me that the failure of the last new Receiver released painful memories to the community.

"But I haven't suffered, Giver. Not really." Jonas smiled. "Oh, I remember the **sunburn** you gave me on the *very* first day. But that wasn't so terrible. What is it that makes you suffer so much? If you gave some of it to me, maybe your pain would be less."

The Giver nodded. "Lie down," he said. "It's time, I suppose. I can't **shield** you forever. You'll have to take it all on **eventually**.

"Let me think," he went on, when Jonas was on the bed, waiting, a little **fearful**.

"All right," The Giver said after a moment, "I've decided. We'll start with something familiar. Let's go once again to a hill, and a sled."

He placed his hands on Jonas's back.

14

It was much the same, this memory, though the hill seemed to be a different one, **steeper**, and the snow was not falling as thickly as it had before.

It was colder, also, Jonas perceived. He could see, as he sat waiting at the top of the hill, that the snow beneath the sled was not thick and soft as it had been before, but hard, and **coat**ed with **bluish** ice.

The sled moved forward, and Jonas grinned with delight, looking forward to the **breathtaking** slide down through the **invigorating** air.

But the runners, this time, couldn't slice through the **frozen expanse** as they had on the other, snow-**cushion**ed hill. They **skitter**ed sideways and the sled gathered speed. Jonas pulled at the rope, trying to **steer**, but the steepness and speed took control from his hands and he was no longer enjoying the feeling of freedom but instead, terrified, was at the **mercy** of the wild **acceleration** downward over the ice.

Sideways, spinning, the **sled** hit a **bump** in the hill and Jonas was **jar**red loose and thrown violently into the air. He fell with his leg twisted under him, and could hear the crack of bone. His face **scrape**d along **jagged** edges of ice and when he came, at last, to a stop, he lay shocked and still, feeling nothing at first but fear.

Then, the first wave of pain. He **gasp**ed. It was as if a **hatchet** lay **lodge**d in his leg, slicing through each **nerve** with a hot **blade**. In his **agony** he perceived the word "fire" and felt flames **lick**ing at the torn bone and flesh. He tried to move, and could not. The pain grew.

He screamed. There was no answer.

Sobbing, he turned his head and **vomit**ed onto the frozen snow. Blood **drip**ped from his face into the vomit.

"Nooooo!" he cried, and the sound disappeared into the empty landscape, into the wind.

Then, suddenly, he was in the Annex room again, **writhing** on the bed. His face was wet with tears.

Able to move now, he rocked his own body back and forth, breathing deeply to release the remembered pain.

He sat, and looked at his own leg, where it lay straight on the bed, unbroken. The **brutal** slice of pain was gone.

But the leg ached horribly, still, and his face felt raw.

"May I have relief-of-pain, please?" he begged. It was always provided in his everyday life for the **bruise**s and **wound**s, for a **mash**ed finger, a stomach ache, a **skin**ned knee from a fall from a bike. There was always a **daub** of **anesthetic ointment**, or a **pill**; or in severe instances, an **injection** that brought complete and **instantaneous deliverance**.

But The Giver said no, and looked away.

Limping, Jonas walked home, pushing his bicycle, that evening. The **sunburn** pain had been so small, in **comparison**, and had not stayed with him. But this ache **linger**ed.

It was not **unendurable**, as the pain on the hill had been. Jonas tried to be brave. He remembered that the Chief Elder had said he was brave.

"Is something wrong, Jonas?" his father asked at the evening meal. "You're so quiet tonight. Aren't you feeling well? Would you like some **medication**?"

But Jonas remembered the rules. No medication for anything related to his training.

And no discussion of his training. At the time for sharing-of-feelings, he simply said that he felt tired, that his school lessons had been unusually demanding that day.

He went to his sleepingroom early, and from behind the closed door he could hear his parents and sister laughing as they gave Gabriel his evening bath.

They have never known pain, he thought. The realization made him feel **desperate**ly lonely, and he rubbed his **throb**bing leg. He eventually slept. Again and again he dreamed of the anguish and the **isolation** on the **forsaken** hill.

The daily training continued, and now it always included pain. The agony of the **fracture**d leg began to seem no more than a mild **discomfort** as The Giver led Jonas firmly, little by little, into the deep and terrible suffering of the past. Each time, in his kindness, The Giver ended the afternoon with a color-filled memory of pleasure: a **brisk sail** on a blue-green lake; a **meadow** dotted with yellow wildflowers; an orange sunset behind mountains.

It was not enough to **assuage** the pain that Jonas was beginning, now, to know.

"*Why*?" Jonas asked him after he had received a **torturous** memory in which he had been **neglect**ed and **unfed**; the hunger had caused **excruciating spasm**s in his empty, **distend**ed stomach. He lay on the bed, aching. "Why do you and I have to hold these memories?"

"It gives us wisdom," The Giver replied. "Without wisdom I could not **fulfill** my function of advising the Committee of Elders when they call upon me."

"But what wisdom do you get from hunger?" Jonas **groan**ed. His stomach still hurt, though the memory had ended.

"Some years ago," The Giver told him, "before your birth, a lot of citizens **petition**ed the Committee of Elders. They wanted to increase the rate of births. They wanted each Birthmother to be **assign**ed four births instead of three, so that the population would increase and there would be more Laborers available."

Jonas nodded, listening. "That makes sense."

"The idea was that certain family units could **accommodate** an additional child."

Jonas nodded again. "Mine could," he pointed out. "We have Gabriel this year, and it's fun, having a third child."

"The Committee of Elders **sought** my advice," The Giver said. "It made sense to them, too, but it was a new idea, and they came to me for wisdom."

"And you used your memories?"

The Giver said yes. "And the strongest memory that came was hunger. It came from many generations back. *Centuries* back. The population had gotten so big that hunger was everywhere. Excruciating hunger and **starvation**. It was followed by **warfare**."

Warfare? It was a concept Jonas did not know. But hunger was familiar to him now. **Unconscious**ly he rubbed his own **abdomen, recall**ing the pain of its **unfulfilled** needs. "So you described that to them?"

"They don't want to hear about pain. They just seek the advice. I simply advised them against increasing the population."

"But you said that that was before my birth. They hardly ever come to you for advice. Only when they—what was it you said? When they have a problem they've never faced before. When did it happen last?"

"Do you remember the day when the plane flew over the community?"

"Yes. I was scared."

"So were they. They prepared to shoot it down. But they sought my advice. I told them to wait."

"But how did you know? How did you know the pilot was lost?"

"I didn't. I used my wisdom, from the memories. I knew that there had been times in the past—terrible times—when people had destroyed others in haste, in fear, and had brought about their own **destruction**."

Jonas realized something. "That means," he said slowly, "that you have memories of destruction. And you have to give them to me, too, because I have to get the wisdom."

The Giver nodded.

"But it will hurt," Jonas said. It wasn't a question.

"It will hurt terribly," The Giver agreed.

"But why can't *everyone* have the memories? I think it would seem a little easier if the memories were shared. You and I wouldn't have to bear so much by ourselves, if everybody took a part."

The Giver sighed. "You're right," he said. "But then everyone would be **burden**ed and pained. They don't want that. And that's the real reason The Receiver is so **vital** to them, and so honored. They selected me—and you—to lift that burden from themselves."

"When did they decide that?" Jonas asked angrily. "It wasn't fair. Let's change it!"

"How do you suggest we do that? I've never been able to think of a way, and I'm supposed to be the one with all the wisdom."

"But there are two of us now," Jonas said **eager**ly. "*Together* we can think of something!"

The Giver watched him with a **wry** smile.

"Why can't we just apply for a change of rules?" Jonas suggested.

The Giver laughed; then Jonas, too, **chuckled** **reluctant**ly.

"The decision was made long before my time or yours," The Giver said, "and before the previous Receiver, and—" He waited.

"Back and back and back." Jonas repeated the familiar phrase. Sometimes it had seemed humorous to him. Sometimes it had seemed **meaningful** and important.

Now it was **ominous**. It meant, he knew, that nothing could be changed.

The newchild, Gabriel, was growing, and successfully passed the tests of **maturity** that the **Nurturer**s gave each month; he could sit alone, now, could reach for and **grasp** small play objects, and he had six teeth. During the daytime hours, Father reported, he was cheerful and seemed of normal intelligence. But he remained **fretful** at night, **whimper**ing often, needing frequent attention.

"After all this extra time I've put in with him," Father said one evening after Gabriel had been **bathe**d and was lying, for the moment, hugging his **hippo placid**ly in the small **crib** that had replaced the basket, "I hope they're not going to decide to release him."

"Maybe it would be for the best," Mother suggested. "I know you don't mind getting up with him at night. But the lack of sleep is awfully hard for me."

"If they release Gabriel, can we get another newchild as a visitor?" asked Lily. She was **kneel**ing beside the crib, making funny faces at the little one, who was smiling back at her.

Jonas's mother rolled her eyes in **dismay**.

"No," Father said, smiling. He **ruffle**d Lily's hair. "It's very rare, anyway, that a newchild's **status** is as uncertain as Gabriel's. It probably won't happen again, for a long time.

"Anyway," he sighed, "they won't make the decision for a while. Right now we're all preparing for a release we'll probably have to make very soon. There's a Birthmother who's expecting twin males next month."

"Oh, dear," Mother said, shaking her head. "If they're **identical**, I hope you're not the one assigned—"

"I am. I'm next on the list. I'll have to select the one to be nurtured, and the one to be released. It's usually not hard, though. Usually it's just a matter of birthweight. We release the smaller of the two."

Jonas, listening, thought suddenly about the bridge and how, standing there, he had wondered what lay Elsewhere. Was there someone there, waiting, who would receive the tiny released twin? Would it grow up Elsewhere, not knowing, ever, that in this community lived a being who looked exactly the same?

For a moment he felt a tiny, **flutter**ing hope that he knew was quite foolish. He hoped that it would be Larissa, waiting. Larissa, the old woman he had bathed. He remembered her **sparkling** eyes, her soft voice, her low chuckle. Fiona had told him recently that Larissa had been released at a wonderful ceremony.

But he knew that the Old were not given children to raise. Larissa's life Elsewhere would be quiet and **serene** as **befit** the Old; she would not welcome the responsibility of nurturing a newchild who needed feeding and care, and would likely cry at night.

"Mother? Father?" he said, the idea coming to him unexpectedly, "why don't we put Gabriel's crib in my room tonight? I know how to feed and comfort him, and it would let you and Father get some sleep."

Father looked doubtful. "You sleep so soundly, Jonas. What if his **restless**ness didn't wake you?"

It was Lily who answered that. "If no one goes to **tend** Gabriel," she pointed out, "he gets very loud. He'd wake *all* of us, if Jonas slept through it."

Father laughed. "You're right, Lily-billy. All right, Jonas, let's try it, just for tonight. I'll take the night off and we'll let Mother get some sleep, too."

Gabriel slept soundly for the earliest part of the night. Jonas, in his bed, lay awake for a while; **from time to time** he raised himself on one elbow, looking over at the crib. The newchild was on his stomach, his arms relaxed beside his head, his eyes closed, and his breathing regular and **undisturbed**. Finally Jonas slept too.

Then, as the middle hours of the night approached, the noise of Gabe's restlessness woke Jonas. The newchild was turning under his cover, **flail**ing his arms, and beginning to whimper.

Jonas rose and went to him. Gently he patted Gabriel's back. Sometimes that was all it took to **lull** him back to sleep. But the newchild still **squirm**ed fretfully under his hand.

Still patting rhythmically, Jonas began to remember the wonderful sail that The Giver had given him not long before: a bright, **breezy** day on a clear turquoise* lake, and above him the white sail of the boat **billow**ing as he moved along in the brisk wind.

He was not aware of giving the memory; but suddenly he realized that it was becoming **dim**mer, that it was sliding through his hand into the being of the newchild. Gabriel became quiet. **Startled**, Jonas pulled back what was left of the memory with a burst of will. He removed his hand from the little back and stood quietly beside the crib.

To himself, he called the memory of the sail forward again. It was still there, but the sky was less blue, the gentle motion of the boat slower, the water of the lake more **murky** and **cloud**ed. He kept it for a while, **soothing** his

* turquoise : 터키석, 터키석 색깔(청록색)을 가진.

own nervousness at what had occurred, then let it go and returned to his bed.

Once more, toward **dawn**, the newchild woke and cried out. Again Jonas went to him. This time he quite **deliberate**ly placed his hand firmly on Gabriel's back, and released the rest of the calming day on the lake. Again Gabriel slept.

But now Jonas lay awake, thinking. He no longer had any more than a **wisp** of the memory, and he felt a small lack where it had been. He could ask The Giver for another sail, he knew. A sail perhaps on ocean, next time, for Jonas had a memory of ocean, now, and knew what it was; he knew that there were sailboats there, too, in memories yet to be **acquire**d.

He wondered, though, if he should confess to The Giver that he had given a memory away. He was not yet qualified to be a Giver himself; nor had Gabriel been selected to be a Receiver.

That he had this power frightened him. He decided not to tell.

15

Jonas entered the Annex room and realized immediately that it was a day when he would be sent away. The Giver was **rigid** in his chair, his face in his hands.

"I'll come back tomorrow, sir," he said quickly. Then he **hesitated**. "Unless maybe there's something I can do to help."

The Giver looked up at him, his face **contort**ed with suffering. "Please," he **gasp**ed, "take some of the pain."

Jonas helped him to his chair at the side of the bed. Then he quickly removed his tunic and lay face down. "Put your hands on me," he directed, aware that in such anguish The Giver might need reminding.

The hands came, and the pain came with them and through them. Jonas **brace**d himself and entered the memory which was **torturing** The Giver.

He was in a confused, noisy, **foul**-smelling place. It was daylight, early morning, and the air was thick with smoke that hung, yellow and brown, above the ground. Around him, everywhere, far across the **expanse** of what seemed to be a field, lay groaning men. A wild-eyed horse, its bridle* torn and **dangling, trot**ted **frantic**ally through the **mound**s of men, **toss**ing its head, **whinny**ing in panic. It **stumble**d, finally, then fell, and did not rise.

Jonas heard a voice next to him. "Water," the voice said in a **parch**ed, **croak**ing whisper.

He turned his head toward the voice and looked into the half-closed eyes of a boy who seemed not much older than himself. Dirt **streak**ed the boy's face and his **matted** blond hair. He lay **sprawl**ed, his gray uniform **glisten**ing with wet, fresh blood.

The colors of the **carnage** were **grotesque**ly bright: the **crimson** wetness on the rough and dusty **fabric**, the **rip**ped **shred**s of grass, startlingly green, in the boy's yellow hair.

The boy stared at him. "Water," he begged again. When he spoke, a new **spurt** of blood **drench**ed the **coarse** cloth across his chest and **sleeve**.

One of Jonas's arms was **immobilize**d with pain, and he

---

* bridle : 말고삐. 말 입에 물리는 재갈의 양 끝에 끈을 장착해서 말의 움직임을 제어하는 데 사용한다.

could see through his own torn sleeve something that looked like **ragged flesh** and **splintery** bone. He tried his remaining arm and felt it move. Slowly he reached to his side, felt the metal container there, and removed its cap, stopping the small motion of his hand **now and then** to wait for the **surging** pain to ease. Finally, when the container was open, he **extend**ed his arm slowly across the blood-soaked earth, inch by inch, and held it to the lips of the boy. Water **trickle**d into the **imploring** mouth and down the **grimy** chin.

The boy sighed. His head fell back, his lower jaw dropping as if he had been surprised by something. A dull **blank**ness slid slowly across his eyes. He was silent.

But the noise continued all around: the cries of the **wound**ed men, the cries begging for water and for Mother and for death. Horses lying on the ground **shriek**ed, raised their heads, and **stab**bed randomly toward the sky with their **hooves**.

From the distance, Jonas could hear the **thud** of **cannons**. **Overwhelm**ed by pain, he lay there in the **fearsome stench** for hours, listened to the men and animals die, and learned what **warfare** meant.

Finally, when he knew that he could bear it no longer and would welcome death himself, he opened his eyes and was once again on the bed.

The Giver looked away, as if he could not bear to see what he had done to Jonas. "Forgive me," he said.

16

Jonas did not want to go back. He didn't want the memories, didn't want the honor, didn't want the wisdom, didn't want the pain. He wanted his childhood again, his scraped knees and ball games. He sat in his **dwelling** alone, watching through the window, seeing children at play, citizens bicycling home from uneventful days at work, **ordinary** lives free of **anguish** because he had been selected, as others before him had, to bear their burden.

But the choice was not his. He returned each day to the **Annex** room.

The Giver was gentle with him for many days following the terrible shared memory of war.

"There are so many good memories," The Giver reminded Jonas. And it was true. By now Jonas had experienced **countless** bits of happiness, things he had never known of before.

He had seen a birthday party, with one child singled out and **celebrate**d on his day, so that now he understood the joy of being an **individual**, special and unique and proud.

He had visited museums and seen paintings filled with all the colors he could now recognize and name.

In one **ecstatic** memory he had ridden a **gleam**ing brown horse across a field that smelled of **damp** grass, and had **dismount**ed beside a small stream from which both he and the horse drank cold, clear water. Now he understood about animals; and in the moment that the horse turned from the stream and **nudge**d Jonas's shoulder **affectionate**ly with its head, he **perceive**d the bonds between animal and human.

He had walked through woods, and sat at night beside a campfire. Although he had through the memories learned about the pain of loss and loneliness, now he gained, too, an understanding of **solitude** and its joy.

"What is your favorite?" Jonas asked The Giver. "You don't have to give it away yet," he added quickly. "Just tell me about it, so I can look forward to it, because I'll have to receive it when your job is done."

The Giver smiled. "Lie down," he said. "I'm happy to give it to you."

Jonas felt the joy of it as soon as the memory began. Sometimes it took a while for him to **get his bearings**, to find his place. But this time he fit right in and felt the happiness that **pervade**d the memory.

He was in a room filled with people, and it was warm, with firelight **glow**ing on a **hearth**. He could see through a window that outside it was night, and snowing. There were colored lights: red and green and yellow, twinkling from a tree which was, oddly, inside the room. On a table, lighted candles stood in a **polish**ed golden holder and cast a soft, **flicker**ing glow. He could smell things cooking, and he heard soft laughter. A golden-haired dog lay sleeping on the floor.

On the floor there were packages wrapped in brightly colored paper and tied with gleaming ribbons. As Jonas watched, a small child began to pick up the packages and pass them around the room: to other children, to adults who were obviously parents, and to an older, quiet couple, man and woman, who sat smiling together on a **couch**.

While Jonas watched, the people began one by one to untie the ribbons on the packages, to unwrap the bright papers, open the boxes and **reveal** toys and clothing and books. There were cries of delight. They hugged one another.

The small child went and sat on the **lap** of the old

woman, and she **rock**ed him and rubbed her cheek against his.

Jonas opened his eyes and lay **contented**ly on the bed, still **luxuriating** in the warm and comforting memory. It had all been there, all the things he had learned to **treasure**.

"What did you perceive?" The Giver asked.

"Warmth," Jonas replied, "and happiness. And—let me think. *Family*. That it was a **celebration** of some sort, a holiday. And something else—I can't quite get the word for it."

"It will come to you."

"Who were the old people? Why were they there?" It had **puzzle**d Jonas, seeing them in the room. The Old of the community did not ever leave their special place, the House of the Old, where they were so well cared for and respected.

"They were called Grandparents."

"Grand parents?"

"Grandparents. It meant parents-of-the-parents, long ago."

"Back and back and back?" Jonas began to laugh. "So actually, there could be parents-of-the-parents-of-the-parents-of-the parents?"

The Giver laughed, too. "That's right. It's a little like looking at yourself looking in a mirror looking at yourself looking in a mirror."

Jonas **frowned**. "But my parents must have had parents! I never thought about it before. Who are my parents-of-the-parents? *Where* are they?"

"You could go look in the Hall of Open Records. You'd find the names. But think, son. If you apply for children, then who will be their parents-of-the-parents? Who will be their grandparents?"

"My mother and father, of course."

"And where will they be?"

Jonas thought. "Oh," he said slowly. "When I finish my training and become a full adult, I'll be given my own dwelling. And then when Lily does, a few years later, she'll get *her* own dwelling, and maybe a **spouse**, and children if she applies for them, and then Mother and Father—"

"That's right."

"As long as they're still working and **contributing** to the community, they'll go and live with the other Childless Adults. And they won't be part of my life anymore.

"And after that, when the time comes, they'll go to the House of the Old," Jonas went on. He was thinking aloud. "And they'll be well cared for, and respected, and when they're **released**, there will be a celebration."

"Which you won't attend," The Giver pointed out.

"No, of course not, because I won't even know about it. By then I'll be so busy with my own life. And Lily will, too.

So our children, if we have them, won't know who their parents-of-parents are, either.

"It seems to work pretty well that way, doesn't it? The way we do it in our community?" Jonas asked. "I just didn't realize there was any other way, until I received that memory."

"It works," The Giver agreed.

Jonas hesitated. "I certainly liked the memory, though. I can see why it's your favorite. I couldn't quite get the word for the whole feeling of it, the feeling that was so strong in the room."

"Love," The Giver told him.

Jonas repeated it. "Love." It was a word and concept new to him.

They were both silent for a minute. Then Jonas said, "Giver?"

"Yes?"

"I feel very foolish saying this. Very, very foolish."

"No need. Nothing is foolish here. Trust the memories and how they make you feel."

"Well," Jonas said, looking at the floor, "I know you don't have the memory anymore, because you gave it to me, so maybe you won't understand this—"

"I will. I am left with a **vague wisp** of that one; and I have many other memories of families, and holidays, and happiness. Of love."

Jonas **blurt**ed out what he was feeling. "I was thinking that . . . well, I can see that it wasn't a very **practical** way to live, with the Old right there in the same place, where maybe they wouldn't be well taken care of, the way they are now, and that we have a better-arranged way of doing things. But anyway, I was thinking, I mean feeling, actually, that it was kind of nice, then. And that I wish we could be that way, and that you could be my grandparent. The family in the memory seemed a little more—" He **falter**ed, not able to find the word he wanted.

"A little more complete," The Giver suggested.

Jonas nodded. "I liked the feeling of love," he **confess**ed. He **glance**d nervously at the speaker on the wall, **reassuring** himself that no one was listening. "I wish we still had that," he whispered. "Of course," he added quickly, "I do understand that it wouldn't work very well. And that it's much better to be organized the way we are now. I can see that it was a *dangerous* way to live."

"What do you mean?"

Jonas hesitated. He wasn't certain, really, what he had meant. He could feel that there was *risk* **involve**d, though he wasn't sure how. "Well," he said finally, grasping for an explanation, "they had *fire* right there in that room. There was a fire burning in the fireplace. And there were candles on a table. I can certainly see why those things were **outlawed**.

"Still," he said slowly, almost to himself, "I did like the light they made. And the warmth."

"Father? Mother?" Jonas asked **tentative**ly after the evening meal. "I have a question I want to ask you."

"What is it, Jonas?" his father asked.

He made himself say the words, though he felt **flush**ed with **embarrass**ment. He had **rehearse**d them in his mind all the way home from the Annex.

"Do you love me?"

There was an **awkward** silence for a moment. Then Father gave a little chuckle. *Jonas.* You, of all people. **Precision** of language, *please!*"

"What do you mean?" Jonas asked. **Amuse**ment was not at all what he had **anticipate**d.

"Your father means that you used a very generalized word, so meaningless that it's become almost **obsolete**," his mother explained carefully.

Jonas stared at them. Meaningless? He had never before felt anything as **meaningful** as the memory.

"And of course our community can't function smoothly if people don't use **precise** language. You could ask, 'Do you enjoy me?' The answer is 'Yes,'" his mother said.

"Or," his father suggested, "'Do you take pride in my **accomplish**ments?' And the answer is **wholeheartedly**

'Yes.'"

"Do you understand why it's **inappropriate** to use a word like 'love'?" Mother asked.

Jonas nodded. "Yes, thank you, I do," he replied slowly.

It was his first lie to his parents.

"Gabriel?" Jonas whispered that night to the newchild. The **crib** was in his room again. After Gabe had **slept soundly** in Jonas's room for four nights, his parents had **pronounce**d the experiment a success and Jonas a hero. Gabriel was growing rapidly, now **crawl**ing and **giggling** across the room and pulling himself up to stand. He could be upgraded in the Nurturing Center, Father said happily, now that he slept; he could be officially named and given to his family in December, which was only two months away.

But when he was taken away, he stopped sleeping again, and cried in the night.

So he was back in Jonas's sleepingroom. They would give it a little more time, they decided. Since Gabe seemed to like it in Jonas's room, he would sleep there at night a little longer, until the habit of sound sleep was fully formed. The Nurturers were very **optimistic** about Gabriel's future.

There was no answer to Jonas's whisper. Gabriel was **sound asleep**.

"Things could change, Gabe," Jonas went on. "Things

could be different. I don't know how, but there must be some way for things to be different. There could be colors.

"And grandparents," he added, staring through the **dim**ness toward the ceiling of his sleepingroom. "And everybody would have the memories.

"You know about memories," he whispered, turning toward the crib.

Gabriel's breathing was **even** and deep. Jonas liked having him there, though he felt **guilty** about the secret. Each night he gave memories to Gabriel: memories of boat rides and picnics in the sun; memories of soft rainfall against **windowpanes**; memories of dancing **bare**foot on a damp **lawn**.

"Gabe?"

The newchild **stir**red slightly in his sleep. Jonas looked over at him.

"There could be love," Jonas whispered.

The next morning, for the first time, Jonas did not take his pill. Something within him, something that had grown there through the memories, told him to throw the pill away.

17

TODAY IS **DECLARED** AN **UNSCHEDULED** HOLIDAY. Jonas, his parents, and Lily all turned in surprise and looked at the wall speaker from which the announcement had come. It happened so **rare**ly, and was such a **treat** for the entire community when it did. Adults were **exempt**ed from the day's work, children from school and training and **volunteer** hours. The **substitute** Laborers, who would be given a different holiday, took over all the necessary tasks: **nurturing**, food delivery, and care of the Old; and the community was free.

Jonas cheered, and put his homework folder down. He had been about to leave for school. School was less important to him now; and before much more time passed, his formal schooling would end. But still, for Twelves, though they had begun their adult training, there were the endless lists of rules to be **memorize**d and the newest technology to be mastered.

He wished his parents, sister, and Gabe a happy day, and rode down the bicycle path, looking for Asher.

He had not taken the **pill**s, now, for four weeks. The **Stirring**s had returned, and he felt a little **guilty** and **embarrassed** about the **pleasurable** dreams that came to him as he slept. But he knew he couldn't go back to the world of no feelings that he had lived in so long.

And his new, **heightene**d feelings **permeate**d a greater **realm** than simply his sleep. Though he knew that his failure to take the pills accounted for some of it, he thought that the feelings came also from the memories. Now he could see all of the colors; and he could *keep* them, too, so that the trees and grass and bushes stayed green in his vision. Gabriel's **rosy** cheeks stayed pink, even when he slept. And apples were always, always red.

Now, through the memories, he had seen oceans and mountain lakes and streams that **gurgle**d through woods; and now he saw the familiar wide river beside the path differently. He saw all of the light and color and history it contained and carried in its slow-moving water; and he knew that there was an Elsewhere from which it came, and an Elsewhere to which it was going.

On this unexpected, casual holiday he felt happy, as he always had on holidays; but with a deeper happiness than ever before. Thinking, as he always did, about **precision** of language, Jonas realized that it was a new ***depth*** of feelings that he was experiencing. Somehow they were not at all the same as the feelings that every evening, in every dwelling, every citizen **analyzed** with endless talk.

"I felt angry because someone broke the play area rules," Lily had said once, making a **fist** with her small hand to **indicate** her **fury**. Her family—Jonas among them—had talked about the possible reasons for rule-breaking, and the need for understanding and **patience**, until Lily's fist had relaxed and her anger was gone.

But Lily had not felt anger, Jonas realized now. **Shallow impatience** and **exasperation**, that was all Lily had felt. He knew that with certainty because now he knew what anger was. Now he had, in the memories, experienced **injustice** and **cruelty**, and he had reacted with **rage** that **welled up** so **passionately** inside him that the thought of discussing it calmly at the evening meal was **unthinkable**.

"I felt sad today," he had heard his mother say, and they had comforted her.

But now Jonas had experienced real sadness. He had felt **grief**. He knew that there was no quick comfort for emotions like those.

These were deeper and they did not need to be told. They were *felt*.

Today, he felt happiness.

"Asher!" He spied his friend's bicycle leaning against a tree at the edge of the playing field. Nearby, other bikes were **strewn** about on the ground. On a holiday the usual rules of order could be **disregard**ed.

He **skid**ded to a stop and dropped his own bike beside the others. "Hey, Ash!" he shouted, looking around. There seemed to be no one in the play area. "Where are you?"

"Psssheeewwww!" A child's voice, coming from behind a nearby bush, made the sound. "Pow! Pow! Pow!"

A female Eleven named Tanya **stagger**ed forward from where she had been hiding. Dramatically she **clutch**ed her stomach and **stumble**d about in a zig-zag pattern, **groan**ing. "You got me!" she called, and fell to the ground, **grin**ning.

"Blam!*"

Jonas, standing on the side of the playing field, recognized Asher's voice. He saw his friend, aiming an **imaginary** weapon in his hand, **dart** from behind one tree to another. "Blam! You're in my line of **ambush**, Jonas! Watch out!"

Jonas stepped back. He moved behind Asher's bike and knelt so that he was out of sight. It was a game he had often played with the other children, a game of good guys

---

* Blam : (의성어) 쾅!

and bad guys, a harmless **pastime** that used up their contained energy and ended only when they all lay **pose**d in **freakish posture**s on the ground.

He had never recognized it before as a game of war.

"Attack!" The shout came from behind the small storehouse where play **equipment** was kept. Three children **dash**ed forward, their imaginary weapons in firing position.

From the opposite side of the field came an opposing shout: "Counter-attack!" From their hiding places a **horde** of children—Jonas recognized Fiona in the group—**emerge**d, running in a **crouch**ed position, firing across the field. Several of them stopped, grabbed their own shoulders and **chest**s with **exaggerate**d gestures, and pretended to be hit. They dropped to the ground and lay **suppress**ing giggles.

Feelings **surge**d within Jonas. He found himself walking forward into the field.

"You're hit, Jonas!" Asher **yell**ed from behind the tree. "Pow! You're hit again!"

Jonas stood alone in the center of the field. Several of the children raised their heads and looked at him uneasily. The attacking armies slowed, emerged from their crouched positions, and watched to see what he was doing.

In his mind, Jonas saw again the face of the boy who had **lain** dying on a field and had begged him for water. He had a sudden **choking** feeling, as if it were difficult to breathe.

One of the children raised an imaginary **rifle** and made an attempt to destroy him with a firing noise. "Pssheeew!" Then they were all silent, standing **awkward**ly, and the only sound was the sound of Jonas's **shudder**ing breaths. He was **struggling** not to cry.

Gradually, when nothing happened, nothing changed, the children looked at each other nervously and went away. He heard the sounds as they righted their bicycles and began to ride down the path that led from the field.

Only Asher and Fiona remained.

"What's wrong, Jonas? It was only a game," Fiona said.

"You **ruin**ed it," Asher said in an **irritate**d voice.

"Don't play it anymore," Jonas **plead**ed.

"I'm the one who's training for Assistant Recreation Director," Asher pointed out angrily. "Games aren't *your* area of **expert**ness."

"**Expertise**," Jonas corrected him automatically.

"Whatever. You can't say what we play, even if you *are* going to be the new Receiver." Asher looked **warily** at him. "I **apologize** for not paying you the respect you **deserve**," he **mumble**d.

"Asher," Jonas said. He was trying to speak carefully, and with kindness, to say exactly what he wanted to say. "You had no way of knowing this. I didn't know it myself until recently. But it's a cruel game. In the past, there have—"

"I said I *apologize*, Jonas."

Jonas sighed. It was no use. Of course Asher couldn't understand. "I accept your **apology**, Asher," he said **wearily**.

"Do you want to go for a ride along the river, Jonas?" Fiona asked, biting her lip with nervousness.

Jonas looked at her. She was so lovely. For a **fleeting** instant he thought he would like nothing better than to ride peacefully along the river path, laughing and talking with his gentle female friend. But he knew that such times had been taken from him now. He shook his head. After a moment his two friends turned and went to their bikes. He watched as they rode away.

Jonas **trudge**d to the bench beside the Storehouse and sat down, **overwhelm**ed with feelings of loss. His childhood, his friendships, his **carefree** sense of security—all of these things seemed to be **slip**ping away. With his new, heightened feelings, he was overwhelmed by sadness at the way the others had laughed and shouted, playing at war. But he knew that they could not understand why, without the memories. He felt such love for Asher and for Fiona. But they could not feel it back, without the memories. And he could not give them those. Jonas knew with certainty that he could change nothing.

Back in their dwelling, that evening, Lily **chatter**ed **merrily** about the wonderful holiday she had had, playing with her friends, having her midday meal out of doors, and (she **confess**ed) **sneak**ing a very short try on her father's bicycle.

"I can't wait till I get my very own bicycle next month. Father's is too big for me. I fell," she explained **matter-of-fact**ly. "Good thing Gabe wasn't in the child seat!"

"A very good thing," Mother agreed, frowning at the idea of it. Gabriel waved his arms at the mention of himself. He had begun to walk just the week before. The first steps of a newchild were always the **occasion** for **celebration** at the Nurturing Center, Father said, but also for the introduction of a **discipline wand**. Now Father brought the **slender** instrument home with him each night, in case Gabriel **misbehave**d.

But he was a happy and **easygoing toddler**. Now he moved **unsteadily** across the room, laughing. "Gay!" he **chirp**ed. "Gay!" It was the way he said his own name.

Jonas **brighten**ed. It had been a **depress**ing day for him, after such a bright start. But he set his **glum** thoughts aside. He thought about starting to teach Lily to ride so that she could speed off proudly after her **Ceremony** of Nine, which would be coming soon. It was hard to believe that it was almost December again, that almost a year had passed since he had become a Twelve.

He smiled as he watched the newchild plant one small foot carefully before the other, grinning with **glee** at his own steps as he tried them out.

"I want to get to sleep early tonight," Father said. "Tomorrow's a busy day for me. The twins are being born tomorrow, and the test results show that they're **identical**."

"One for here, one for Elsewhere," Lily **chant**ed. "One for here, one for Else—"

"Do you actually *take* it Elsewhere, Father?" Jonas asked.

"No, I just have to make the selection. I weigh them, hand the larger over to a Nurturer who's standing by, waiting, and then I get the smaller one all cleaned up and **comfy**. Then I perform a small Ceremony of Release and—" He glanced down, grinning at Gabriel. "Then I wave bye-bye," he said, in the special sweet voice he used when he spoke to the newchild. He waved his hand in the familiar gesture.

Gabriel giggled and waved bye-bye back to him. "And somebody else comes to get him? Somebody from Elsewhere?"

"That's right, Jonas-bonus."

Jonas rolled his eyes in embarrassment that his father had used the silly pet name.

Lily was deep in thought. "What if they give the little twin a name Elsewhere, a name like, oh, maybe Jonathan?

And here, in our community, at his naming, the twin that we kept here is given the name Jonathan, and then there would be two children with the same name, and they would *look* exactly the same, and someday, maybe when they were a Six, one group of Sixes would go to visit another community on a bus, and there in the other community, in the *other* group of Sixes, would be a Jonathan who was exactly the same as the *other* Jonathan, and then maybe they would get mixed up and take the wrong Jonathan home, and maybe his parents wouldn't notice, and then—"

She paused for breath.

"Lily," Mother said, "I have a wonderful idea. Maybe when you become a Twelve, they'll give you the **Assign**ment of Storyteller! I don't think we've had a Storyteller in the community for a long time. But if I were on the **Committee**, I would **definite**ly choose you for that job!"

Lily grinned. "I have a *better* idea for one more story," she announced. "What if actually we were *all* twins and didn't know it, and so Elsewhere there would be another Lily, and another Jonas, and another Father, and another Asher, and another Chief **Elder**, and another—"

Father groaned. "Lily," he said. "It's bedtime."

18

"Giver," Jonas asked the next afternoon, "Do you ever think about release?"

"Do you mean my own release, or just the general topic of release?"

"Both, I guess. I apologi—I mean I should have been more **precise**. But I don't know exactly what I meant."

"Sit back up. No need to lie down while we're talking." Jonas, who had already been stretched out on the bed when the question came to his mind, sat back up.

"I guess I do think about it **occasionally**," The Giver said. "I think about my own release when I'm in an awful lot of pain. I wish I could put in a request for it, sometimes. But I'm not **permitted** to do that until the new Receiver is trained."

"Me," Jonas said in a **dejected** voice. He was not looking forward to the end of the training, when he would become the new Receiver. It was clear to him what a terribly difficult and lonely life it was, despite the honor.

"I can't request release either," Jonas pointed out. "It was in my rules."

The Giver laughed **harshly**. "I know that. They **hammered out** those rules after the failure ten years ago."

Jonas had heard again and again now, **reference** to the previous failure. But he still did not know what had happened ten years before. "Giver," he said, "tell me what happened. Please."

The Giver **shrugged**. "On the surface, it was quite simple. A Receiver-to-be was selected, the way you were. The selection went smoothly enough. The Ceremony was held, and the selection was made. The crowd cheered, as they did for you. The new Receiver was puzzled and a little **frighten**ed, as you were."

"My parents told me it was a female."

The Giver nodded.

Jonas thought of his favorite female, Fiona, and **shiver**ed. He wouldn't want his gentle friend to suffer the way he had, taking on the memories. "What was she like?" he asked The Giver.

The Giver looked sad, thinking about it. "She was a **remarkable** young woman. Very **self-possessed** and **serene**.

Intelligent, **eager** to learn." He shook his head and drew a deep breath. "You know, Jonas, when she came to me in this room, when she presented herself to begin her training—"

Jonas interrupted him with a question. "Can you tell me her name? My parents said that it wasn't to be spoken again in the community. But couldn't you say it just to me?"

The Giver **hesitate**d painfully, as if saying the name aloud might be **excruciating**. "Her name was Rosemary," he told Jonas, finally.

"Rosemary. I like that name."

The Giver went on. "When she came to me for the first time, she sat there in the chair where you sat on your first day. She was eager and excited and a little scared. We talked. I tried to explain things as well as I could."

"The way you did to me."

The Giver **chuckle**d **ruefully**. "The explanations are difficult. The whole thing is so beyond one's experience. But I tried. And she listened carefully. Her eyes were very **luminous**, I remember."

He looked up suddenly. "Jonas, I gave you a memory that I told you was my favorite. I still have a **shred** of it left. The room, with the family, and grandparents?"

Jonas nodded. Of course he remembered. "Yes," he said. "It had that wonderful feeling with it. You told me it was love."

"You can understand, then, that that's what I felt for Rosemary," The Giver explained. "I loved her.

"I feel it for you, too," he added.

"What happened to her?" Jonas asked.

"Her training began. She received well, as you do. She was so **enthusiastic**. So delighted to experience new things. I remember her laughter . . ."

His voice **falter**ed and **trail**ed **off**.

"What happened?" Jonas asked again, after a moment. "Please tell me."

The Giver closed his eyes. "It broke my heart, Jonas, to **transfer** pain to her. But it was my job. It was what I had to do, the way I've had to do it to you."

The room was silent. Jonas waited. Finally The Giver continued.

"Five weeks. That was all. I gave her happy memories: a ride on a merry-go-round; a **kitten** to play with; a picnic. Sometimes I chose one just because I knew it would make her laugh, and I so **treasure**d the sound of that laughter in this room that had always been so silent.

"But she was like you, Jonas. She wanted to experience everything. She knew that it was her responsibility. And so she asked me for more difficult memories."

Jonas held his breath for a moment. "You didn't give her *war*, did you? Not after just five weeks?"

The Giver shook his head and sighed. "No. And I didn't give her physical pain. But I gave her loneliness. And I gave her loss. I transferred a memory of a child taken from its parents. That was the first one. She appeared **stunned** at its end."

Jonas **swallowed**. Rosemary, and her laughter, had begun to seem real to him, and he pictured her looking up from the bed of memories, shocked.

The Giver continued. "I backed off, gave her more little delights. But everything changed, once she knew about pain. I could see it in her eyes."

"She wasn't brave enough?" Jonas suggested.

The Giver didn't respond to the question. "She insisted that I continue, that I not **spare** her. She said it was her duty. And I knew, of course, that she was correct.

"I couldn't bring myself to **inflict** physical pain on her. But I gave her anguish of many kinds. **Poverty**, and hunger, and terror.

"I *had* to, Jonas. It was my job. And she had been chosen." The Giver looked at him **imploringly**. Jonas **stroked** his hand.

"Finally one afternoon, we finished for the day. It had been a hard **session**. I tried to finish—as I do with you—by transferring something happy and cheerful. But the times of laughter were gone by then. She stood up very silently, frowning, as if she were making a decision. Then she came over to me and put her arms around me. She kissed my cheek." As Jonas watched, The Giver stroked his own cheek, **recall**ing the touch of Rosemary's lips ten years before.

"She left here that day, left this room, and did not go back to her dwelling. I was **notified** by the Speaker that she had gone directly to the Chief Elder and asked to be released."

"But it's against the rules! The Receiver-in-training can't apply for rel—"

"It's in your rules, Jonas. But it wasn't in hers. She asked for release, and they had to give it to her. I never saw her again."

So that was the failure, Jonas thought. It was obvious that it saddened The Giver very deeply. But it didn't seem such a terrible thing, after all. And he, Jonas, would never have done it—never have requested release, no matter how difficult his training became. The Giver needed a **successor**, and he had been chosen.

A thought occurred to Jonas. Rosemary had been released very early in her training. What if something happened to him, Jonas? He had a whole year's worth of memories now.

"Giver," he asked, "I can't request release, I know that. But what if something happened: an accident? What if I fell into the river like the little Four, Caleb, did? Well, that doesn't make sense because I'm a good swimmer. But what if I couldn't swim, and fell into the river and was lost? Then there wouldn't be a new Receiver, but you would already have given away an awful lot of important memories, so even though they would select a new Receiver, the memories would be gone except for the shreds that you have left of them? And then what if—"

He started to laugh, suddenly. "I sound like my sister, Lily," he said, **amuse**d at himself.

The Giver looked at him **gravel**y. "You just stay away from the river, my friend," he said. "The community lost Rosemary after five weeks and it was a **disaster** for them. I don't know *what* the community would do if they lost you."

"Why was it a disaster?"

"I think I mentioned to you once," The Giver reminded him, "that when she was gone, the memories came back to the people. If you were to be lost in the river, Jonas, your memories would not be lost with you. Memories are *forever*.

"Rosemary had only those five weeks worth, and most of them were good ones. But there were those few terrible memories, the ones that had **overwhelm**ed her. For a while they overwhelmed the community. All those *feelings!* They'd never experienced that before. "I was so **devastate**d by my own **grief** at her loss, and my own feeling of failure, that I didn't even try to help them through it. I was angry, too."

The Giver was quiet for a moment, obviously thinking. "You know," he said, finally, "if they lost *you*, with all the training you've had now, they'd have all those memories again themselves."

Jonas **made a face**. "They'd hate that."

"They certainly would. They wouldn't know how to deal with it at all."

"The only way I deal with it is by having you there to help me," Jonas pointed out with a sigh.

The Giver nodded. "I suppose," he said slowly, "that I could—"

"You could what?"

The Giver was still deep in thought. After a moment, he said, "If you **float**ed off in the river, I suppose I could help the whole community the way I've helped you. It's an interesting concept. I need to think about it some more. Maybe we'll talk about it again sometime. But not now.

"I'm glad you're a good swimmer, Jonas. But stay away from the river." He laughed a little, but the laughter was not **lighthearted**. His thoughts seemed to be elsewhere, and his eyes were very troubled.

19

Jonas **glanced** at the clock. There was so much work to be done, always, that he and The Giver **seldom** simply sat and talked, the way they just had.

"I'm sorry that I wasted so much time with my questions," Jonas said. "I was only asking about **release** because my father is releasing a newchild today. A twin. He has to select one and release the other one. They do it by weight." Jonas glanced at the clock. "Actually, I suppose he's already finished. I think it was this morning."

The Giver's face took on a **solemn** look. "I wish they wouldn't do that," he said quietly, almost to himself.

"Well, they can't have two **identical** people around! Think how confusing it would be!" Jonas **chuckled**.

"I wish I could watch," he added, as an afterthought. He liked the thought of seeing his father perform the ceremony, and making the little twin clean and comfy. His father was such a gentle man.

"You can watch," The Giver said.

"No," Jonas told him. "They never let children watch. It's very private."

"Jonas," The Giver told him, "I know that you read your training instructions very carefully. Don't you remember that you are allowed to ask anyone anything?"

Jonas nodded. "Yes, but—"

"Jonas, when you and I have finished our time together, you will be the new Receiver. You can read the books; you'll have the memories. You have access to *everything*. It's part of your training. If you want to watch a release, you have simply to ask."

Jonas shrugged. "Well, maybe I will, then. But it's too late for this one. I'm sure it was this morning."

The Giver told him, then, something he had not known. "All private ceremonies are recorded. They're in the Hall of Closed Records. *Do you want to see this morning's release?*"

Jonas hesitated. He was afraid that his father wouldn't like it, if he watched something so private.

"I think you should," The Giver told him firmly.

"All right, then," Jonas said. "Tell me how."

The Giver rose from his chair, went to the speaker on

the wall, and **clicked** the switch from OFF to ON.

The voice spoke immediately. "Yes, Receiver. How may I help you?"

"I would like to see this morning's release of the twin."

"One moment, Receiver. Thank you for your instructions."

Jonas watched the video screen above the row of switches. Its **blank** face began to **flicker** with zig-zag lines; then some numbers appeared, followed by the date and time. He was **astonish**ed and delighted that this was available to him, and surprised that he had not known.

Suddenly he could see a small windowless room, empty except for a bed, a table with some **equipment** on it—Jonas recognized a **scale**; he had seen them before, when he'd been doing **volunteer** hours at the Nurturing Center—and a **cupboard**. He could see pale **carpeting** on the floor.

"It's just an **ordinary** room," he commented. "I thought maybe they'd have it in the **Auditorium**, so that everybody could come. All the Old go to Ceremonies of Release. But I suppose that when it's just a newborn, they don't—"

"Shhh," The Giver said, his eyes on the screen.

Jonas's father, wearing his nurturing uniform, entered the room, **cradling** a tiny newchild wrapped in a soft **blanket** in his arms. A uniformed woman followed through the door, carrying a second newchild wrapped in a similar blanket.

"That's my father." Jonas found himself whispering, as if he might wake the little ones if he spoke aloud. "And the other Nurturer is his assistant. She's still in training, but she'll be finished soon."

The two Nurturers unwrapped the blankets and laid the identical newborns on the bed. They were **naked**. Jonas could see that they were males.

He watched, **fascinate**d, as his father gently lifted one and then the other to the scale and weighed them.

He heard his father laugh. "Good," his father said to the woman. "I thought for a moment that they might both be exactly the same. *Then* we'd have a problem. But this one," he handed one, after rewrapping it, to his assistant, "is six **pound**s **even**. So you can clean him up and dress him and take him over to the Center."

The woman took the newchild and left through the door she had entered.

Jonas watched as his father bent over the **squirm**ing newchild on the bed. "And you, little guy, you're only five pounds ten ounces. A *shrimp*!*"

"That's the special voice he uses with Gabriel," Jonas

* shrimp : 원래는 '작은 새우'를 뜻하지만 의미가 파생하여 '난쟁이, 꼬마, 왜소한 사람'을 지칭하기도 한다.

remarked, smiling.

"Watch," The Giver said.

"Now he cleans him up and makes him comfy," Jonas told him. "He told me."

"Be quiet, Jonas," The Giver commanded in a strange voice. "*Watch.*"

Obediently Jonas **concentrate**d on the screen, waiting for what would happen next. He was especially curious about the ceremony part.

His father turned and opened the cupboard. He took out a **syringe** and a small bottle. Very carefully he **insert**ed the needle into the bottle and began to fill the syringe with a clear liquid.

Jonas **winced** **sympathetic**ally. He had forgotten that newchildren had to get shots. He hated shots himself, though he knew that they were necessary.

To his surprise, his father began very carefully to direct the needle into the top of newchild's **forehead**, **puncturing** the place where the **fragile** skin **pulse**d. The newborn squirmed, and **wail**ed faintly.

"Why's he—"

"Shhh," The Giver said sharply.

His father was talking, and Jonas realized that he was hearing the answer to the question he had started to ask. Still in the special voice, his father was saying, "I know, I know. It hurts, little guy. But I have to use a **vein**, and the veins in your arms are still too teeny-weeny.*"

He pushed the plunger■ very slowly, **inject**ing the liquid into the **scalp** vein until the syringe was empty.

"All done. That wasn't so hard, was it?" Jonas heard his father say cheerfully. He turned aside and dropped the syringe into a waste **receptacle.**

Now he cleans him up and makes him comfy, Jonas said to himself, aware that The Giver didn't want to talk during the little ceremony.

As he continued to watch, the newchild, no longer crying, moved his arms and legs in a **jerk**ing motion. Then he went **limp**. His head fell to the side, his eyes half open. Then he was still.

With an odd, shocked feeling, Jonas recognized the gestures and **posture** and expression. They were familiar.

He had seen them before. But he couldn't remember where. Jonas stared at the screen, waiting for something to happen. But nothing did. The little twin lay motionless. His father was putting things away. Folding the blanket. Closing the cupboard.

---

* teeny-weeny: (= tiny) 작은, 조그마한.

■ plunger : 플런저. 피스톤의 내용물을 밀어내는 기기, 혹은 손잡이 끝에 흡착 고무판이 붙어 있어 배관을 뚫는 용구. 여기서는 주사기에서 주사통 속의 약물을 주입하기 위해 밀어 넣는 부분을 말한다.

Once again, as he had on the playing field, he felt the **choking** sensation. Once again he saw the face of the light-haired, bloodied soldier as life left his eyes. The memory came back.

He killed it! My father killed it! Jonas said to himself, **stun**ned at what he was realizing. He continued to stare at the screen **numb**ly.

His father **tidied** the room. Then he picked up a small **carton** that lay waiting on the floor, set it on the bed, and lifted the limp body into it. He placed the **lid** on tightly.

He picked up the carton and carried it to the other side of the room. He opened a small door in the wall; Jonas could see darkness behind the door. It seemed to be the same sort of **chute** into which trash was **deposit**ed at school.

His father **load**ed the carton containing the body into the chute and gave it a **shove**.

"Bye-bye, little guy," Jonas heard his father say before he left the room. Then the screen went blank.

The Giver turned to him. Quite calmly, he related, "When the Speaker notified me that Rosemary had applied for release, they turned on the tape to show me the process. There she was—my last **glimpse** of that beautiful child—waiting. They brought in the syringe and asked her to roll up her **sleeve**.

"You suggested, Jonas, that perhaps she wasn't brave enough? I don't know about **bravery**: what it is, what it means. I do know that I sat here numb with horror. **Wretched** with helplessness. And I listened as Rosemary told them that she would prefer to inject herself.

"Then she did so. I didn't watch. I looked away."

The Giver turned to him. "Well, there you are, Jonas. You were wondering about release," he said in a **bitter** voice.

Jonas felt a **ripping** sensation inside himself, the feeling of terrible pain **clawing** its way forward to **emerge** in a cry.

20

"I won't! I won't go home! You can't make me!" Jonas **sob**bed and shouted and **pound**ed the bed with his **fists**.

"Sit up, Jonas," The Giver told him firmly.

Jonas **obey**ed him. **Weeping**, **shudder**ing, he sat on the edge of the bed. He would not look at The Giver.

"You may stay here tonight. I want to talk to you. But you must be quiet now, while I **notify** your family unit. No one must hear you cry."

Jonas looked up wildly. "No one heard that little twin cry, either! No one but my father!" He **collapse**d in sobs again.

The Giver waited silently. Finally Jonas was able to quiet himself and he sat **huddle**d, his shoulders shaking.

The Giver went to the wall speaker and **click**ed the switch to ON.

"Yes, Receiver. How may I help you?"

"Notify the new Receiver's family unit that he will be staying with me tonight, for additional training."

"I will take care of that, sir. Thank you for your instructions," the voice said.

"I will take care of that, sir. I will take care of that, sir," Jonas **mimic**ked in a **cruel, sarcastic** voice. "I will do whatever you like, sir. I will kill people, sir. Old people? Small newborn people? I'd be happy to kill them, sir. Thank you for your instructions, sir. How may I help y—" He couldn't seem to stop.

The Giver **grasp**ed his shoulders firmly. Jonas fell silent and stared at him.

"Listen to me, Jonas. They can't help it. *They know nothing*."

"You said that to me once before."

"I said it because it's true. It's the way they live. It's the life that was created for them. It's the same life that you would have, if you had not been chosen as my **successor**."

"But he *lied* to me!" Jonas wept.

"It's what he was told to do, and he knows nothing else."

"What about you? Do *you* lie to me, too?" Jonas almost **spat** the question at The Giver.

"I am **empower**ed to lie. But I have never lied to you."

Jonas stared at him. "**Release** is always like that? For people who break the rules three times? For the *Old*? Do they kill the Old, too?"

"Yes, it's true."

"And what about Fiona? She loves the Old! She's in training to care for them. Does she know yet? What will she do when she finds out? How will she feel?" Jonas brushed wetness from his face with the back of one hand.

"Fiona is already being trained in the fine art of release," The Giver told him. "She's very **efficient** at her work, your red-haired friend. Feelings are not part of the life she's learned."

Jonas wrapped his arms around himself and **rock**ed his own body back and forth. "What should I do? I can't go back! I can't!"

The Giver stood up. "First, I will order our evening meal. Then we will eat."

Jonas found himself using the **nasty**, sarcastic voice again. "Then we'll have a sharing of feelings?"

The Giver gave a **rueful**, **anguish**ed, empty laugh. "Jonas, you and I are the only ones who *have* feelings. We've been sharing them now for almost a year."

"I'm sorry, Giver," Jonas said miserably. "I don't mean to be so hateful. Not to you."

The Giver rubbed Jonas's **hunch**ed shoulders. "And

after we eat," he went on, "we'll make a plan."

Jonas looked up, **puzzled**. "A plan for what? There's nothing. There's nothing we can do. It's always been this way. Before me, before you, before the ones who came before you. Back and back and back." His voice **trail**ed the familiar **phrase**.

"Jonas," The Giver said, after a moment, "it's true that it has been this way for what seems forever. But the memories tell us that it has not *always* been. People felt things once. You and I have been part of that, so we know. We know that they once felt things like pride, and sorrow, and—"

"And love," Jonas added, remembering the family scene that had so affected him. "And pain." He thought again of the soldier.

"The worst part of holding the memories is not the pain. It's the loneliness of it. Memories need to be shared."

"I've started to share them with you," Jonas said, trying to cheer him.

"That's true. And having you here with me over the past year has made me realize that things must change. For years I've felt that they should, but it seemed so hopeless.

"Now for the first time I think there might be a way," The Giver said slowly. "And you brought it to my attention, **barely**—" He glanced at the clock. "two hours ago."

Jonas watched him, and listened.

It was late at night, now. They had talked and talked. Jonas sat wrapped in a **robe belong**ing to The Giver, the long robe that only **Elder**s wore.

It was possible, what they had planned. Barely possible. If it failed, he would very likely be killed.

But what did that matter? If he stayed, his life was no longer worth living.

"Yes," he told The Giver. "I'll do it. I think I can do it. I'll try, anyway. But I want you to come with me."

The Giver shook his head. "Jonas," he said, "the community has **depend**ed, all these generations, back and back and back, on a **resident** Receiver to hold their memories for them. I've turned over many of them to you in the past year. And I can't take them back. There's no way for me to get them back if I have given them.

"So if you escape, once you are gone—and, Jonas, you know that you can never return—"

Jonas nodded **solemnl**y. It was the **terrify**ing part. "Yes," he said, "I know. But if you come with me—"

The Giver shook his head and made a gesture to silence him. He continued. "If you get away, if you get beyond, if you get to Elsewhere, it will mean that the community has to bear the **burden** themselves, of the memories you had been holding for them.

"I think that they can, and that they will **acquire** some wisdom. But it will be **desperate**ly hard for them. When we lost Rosemary ten years ago, and her memories returned to the people, they panicked. And those were such few memories, compared to yours. When your memories return, they'll need help. Remember how I helped you in the beginning, when the receiving of memories was new to you?"

Jonas nodded. "It was scary at first. And it hurt a lot."

"You needed me then. And now they will."

"It's no use. They'll find someone to take my place. They'll choose a new Receiver."

"There's no one ready for training, not right away. Oh, they'll speed up the selection, of course. But I can't think of another child who has the right qualities—"

"There's a little female with pale eyes. But she's only a Six."

"That's correct. I know the one you mean. Her name is Katharine. But she's too young. So they will be *forced* to bear those memories."

"I want you to come, Giver," Jonas **plead**ed.

"No. I have to stay here," The Giver said firmly. "I want to, Jonas. If I go with you, and together we take away *all* their protection from the memories, Jonas, the community will be left with no one to help them. They'll be thrown into chaos. They'll destroy themselves. I can't go."

"Giver," Jonas suggested, "you and I don't need to *care* about the rest of them."

The Giver looked at him with a **questioning** smile. Jonas hung his head. Of course they needed to care. It was the meaning of everything.

"And in any case, Jonas," The Giver sighed, "I wouldn't make it. I'm very weakened now. Do you know that I no longer see colors?"

Jonas's heart broke. He reached for The Giver's hand.

"You have the colors," The Giver told him. "And you have the courage. I will help you to have the strength."

"A year ago," Jonas reminded him, "when I had just become a Twelve, when I began to see the first color, you told me that the beginning had been different for you. But that I wouldn't understand."

The Giver **brighten**ed. "That's true. And do you know, Jonas, that with all your knowledge now, with all your memories, with all you've learned—*still* you won't understand? Because I've been a little selfish. I haven't given any of it to you. I wanted to keep it for myself to the last."

"Keep what?"

"When I was just a boy, younger than you, it began to come to me. But it wasn't the seeing-beyond for me. It was different. For me, it was *hearing*-beyond."

Jonas **frowned**, trying to figure that out. "What did you hear?" he asked.

"Music," The Giver said, smiling. "I began to hear something truly **remarkable**, and it is called music. I'll give you some before I go."

Jonas shook his head **emphatically**. "No, Giver," he said. "I want you to keep that, to have with you, when I'm gone."

Jonas went home the next morning, cheerfully greeted his parents, and lied easily about what a busy, pleasant night he had had.

His father smiled and lied easily, too, about his busy and pleasant day the day before.

Throughout the school day, as he did his lessons, Jonas went over the plan in his head. It seemed **startlingly** simple. Jonas and The Giver had gone over it and over it, late into the night hours.

For the next two weeks, as the time for the December **Ceremony** approached, The Giver would **transfer** every memory of courage and strength that he could to Jonas. He would need those to help him find the Elsewhere that they were both sure existed. They knew it would be a very difficult journey.

Then, in the middle of the night before the Ceremony, Jonas would secretly leave his **dwelling**. This was probably the most dangerous part, because it was a **violation** of a major rule for any citizen not on official business to leave a dwelling at night.

"I'll leave at midnight," Jonas said. "The Food Collectors will be finished picking up the evening-meal remains by then, and the Path-Maintenance Crews don't start their work that early. So there won't be anyone to see me, unless of course someone is out on **emergency** business."

"I don't know what you should do if you are seen, Jonas," The Giver had said. "I have memories, of course, of all kinds of escapes. People **flee**ing from terrible things throughout history. But every situation is **individual**. There is no memory of one like this."

"I'll be careful," Jonas said. "No one will see me."

"As Receiver-in-training, you're held in very high respect already. So I think you wouldn't be questioned very **forcefully**."

"I'd just say I was on some important **errand** for the Receiver. I'd say it was all your fault that I was out after hours," Jonas **tease**d.

They both laughed a little nervously. But Jonas was certain that he could **slip** away, unseen, from his house, carrying an extra set of clothing. Silently he would take his bicycle to the **riverbank** and leave it there hidden in bushes with the clothing folded beside it.

Then he would make his way through the darkness, on foot, silently, to the **Annex**.

"There's no nighttime **attendant**," The Giver explained. "I'll leave the door unlocked. You simply slip into the room. I'll be waiting for you."

His parents would discover, when they woke, that he was gone. They would also find a cheerful note from Jonas on his bed, telling them that he was going for an early morning ride along the river; that he would be back for the Ceremony.

His parents would be **irritate**d but not **alarm**ed. They would think him **inconsiderate** and they would plan to **chastise** him, later.

They would wait, with **mount**ing anger, for him; finally they would be forced to go, taking Lily to the Ceremony without him.

"They won't say anything to anyone, though," Jonas said, quite certain. "They won't call attention to my rudeness because it would **reflect** on their parenting. And anyway, everyone is so **involve**d in the Ceremony that they probably won't notice that I'm not there. Now that I'm a Twelve and in training, I don't have to sit with my age group any more. So Asher will think I'm with my parents, or with you—"

"And your parents will **assume** you're with Asher, or with me—"

Jonas **shrugged**. "It will take everyone a while to realize that I'm not there at all."

"And you and I will be long on our way by then."

In the early morning, The Giver would order a **vehicle** and driver from the Speaker. He visited the other communities frequently, meeting with their Elders; his responsibilities **extend**ed over all the surrounding areas. So this would not be an unusual **undertaking**.

Ordinarily The Giver did not attend the December Ceremony. Last year he had been present because of the **occasion** of Jonas's selection, in which he was so involved. But his life was usually quite separate from that of the community. No one would comment on his absence, or on the fact that he had chosen this day to be away.

When the driver and vehicle arrived, The Giver would send the driver on some brief errand. During his absence, The Giver would help Jonas hide in the storage area of the vehicle. He would have with him a **bundle** of food which The Giver would save from his own meals during the next two weeks.

The Ceremony would begin, with all the community there, and by then Jonas and The Giver would be on their way.

By midday Jonas's absence would become **apparent**, and would be a cause for serious concern. The Ceremony would not be **disrupt**ed—such a disruption would be **unthinkable**. But searchers would be sent out into the community.

By the time his bicycle and clothing were found, The Giver would be returning. Jonas, by then, would be on his own, making his journey Elsewhere.

The Giver, on his return, would find the community in a state of confusion and panic. **Confront**ed by a situation which they had never faced before, and having no memories from which to find either **solace** or wisdom, they would not know what to do and would seek his advice.

He would go to the **Auditorium** where the people would be gathered, still. He would **stride** to the stage and command their attention.

He would make the solemn announcement that Jonas had been lost in the river. He would immediately begin the Ceremony of Loss.

"Jonas, Jonas," they would say loudly, as they had once said the name of Caleb. The Giver would lead the **chant**. Together they would let Jonas's presence in their lives fade away as they said his name **in unison** more slowly, softer and softer, until he was disappearing from them, until he was no more than an occasional **murmur** and then, by the end of the long day, gone forever, not to be mentioned again.

Their attention would turn to the **overwhelming** task of bearing the memories themselves. The Giver would help them.

"Yes, I understand that they'll need you," Jonas had said at the end of the **lengthy** discussion and planning. "But I'll need you, too. Please come with me." He knew the answer even as he made the final **plea**.

"My work will be finished," The Giver had replied gently, "when I have helped the community to change and become whole.

"I'm **grateful** to you, Jonas, because without you I would never have **figured out** a way to bring about the change. But your role now is to escape. And my role is to stay."

"But don't you *want* to be with me, Giver?" Jonas asked sadly.

The Giver hugged him. "I love you, Jonas," he said. "But I have another place to go. When my work here is finished, I want to be with my daughter."

Jonas had been staring **glum**ly at the floor. Now he looked up, startled. "I didn't know you had a daughter,

Giver! You told me that you'd had a **spouse**. But I never knew about your daughter."

The Giver smiled, and nodded. For the first time in their long months together, Jonas saw him look truly happy.

"Her name was Rosemary," The Giver said.

21

It would work. They could make it work, Jonas told himself again and again throughout the day.

But that evening everything changed. All of it—all the things they had thought through so **meticulous**ly—fell apart.

That night, Jonas was forced to **flee**. He left the dwelling shortly after the sky became dark and the community still. It was terribly dangerous because some of the work crews were still about, but he moved **stealthily** and silently, staying in the shadows, making his way past the darkened dwellings and the empty Central Plaza, toward the river. Beyond the Plaza he could see the House of the Old, with the Annex behind it, outlined against the night sky. But he could not stop there. There was no time. Every minute counted now, and every minute must take him farther from the community.

Now he was on the bridge, hunched over on the bicycle, **pedal**ing **steadily**. He could see the dark, **churn**ing water far below.

He felt, surprisingly, no fear, nor any regret at leaving the community behind. But he felt a very deep sadness that he had left his closest friend behind. He knew that in the danger of his escape he must be absolutely silent; but with his heart and mind, he called back and hoped that with his **capacity** for hearing-beyond, The Giver would know that Jonas had said goodbye.

It had happened at the evening meal. The family unit was eating together as always: Lily **chatter**ing away, Mother and Father making their **customary** comments (and lies, Jonas knew) about the day. Nearby, Gabriel played happily on the floor, **babbling** his baby talk, looking with **glee now and then** toward Jonas, obviously delighted to have him back after the unexpected night away from the dwelling.

Father **glance**d down toward the **toddler**. "Enjoy it, little guy," he said. "This is your last night as visitor."

"What do you mean?" Jonas asked him.

Father sighed with disappointment. "Well, you know he wasn't here when you got home this morning because we had him stay overnight at the **Nurturing** Center. It seemed like a good opportunity, with you gone, to give it a try. He'd been **sleep**ing so **soundly**."

"Didn't it go well?" Mother asked **sympathetic**ally.

Father gave a rueful laugh. "That's an understatement. It was a **disaster**. He cried all night, apparently. The night crew couldn't handle it. They were *really* **frazzled** by the time I got to work."

"Gabe, you **naughty** thing," Lily said, with a **scold**ing little **cluck** toward the **grin**ning toddler on the floor.

"So," Father went on, "we obviously had to make the decision. Even I **vote**d for Gabriel's release when we had the meeting this afternoon."

Jonas put down his fork and stared at his father. "Release?" he asked.

Father nodded. "We certainly gave it our best try, didn't we?"

"Yes, we did," Mother agreed **emphatic**ally.

Lily nodded in agreement, too.

Jonas worked at keeping his voice absolutely calm. "When?" he asked. "When will he be released?"

"First thing tomorrow morning. We have to start our preparations for the Naming **Ceremony**, so we thought we'd get this taken care of right away.

"It's bye-bye to you, Gabe, in the morning," Father had

said, in his sweet, sing-song voice.

Jonas reached the opposite side of the river, stopped briefly, and looked back. The community where his entire life had been lived lay behind him now, sleeping. At **dawn**, the orderly, **disciplined** life he had always known would continue again, without him. The life where nothing was ever unexpected. Or **inconvenient**. Or unusual. The life without color, pain, or past.

He pushed firmly again at the pedal with his foot and continued riding along the road. It was not safe to spend time looking back. He thought of the rules he had broken so far: enough that if he were caught, now, he would be **condemned**.

First, he had left the dwelling at night. A major **transgression**.

Second, he had robbed the community of food: a very serious crime, even though what he had taken was **leftovers**, set out on the dwelling doorsteps for collection.

Third, he had stolen his father's bicycle. He had **hesitated** for a moment, standing beside the bike**port** in the darkness, not wanting anything of his father's and uncertain, as well, whether he could comfortably ride the larger bike when he was so **accustomed** to his own.

But it was necessary because it had the child seat

attached to the back.

And he had taken Gabriel, too.

He could feel the little head **nudge** his back, bouncing gently against him as he rode. Gabriel was sleeping soundly, **strap**ped into the seat. Before he had left the dwelling, he had laid his hands firmly on Gabe's back and **transmit**ted to him the most **soothing** memory he could: a slow-swinging hammock* under palm trees on an island someplace, at evening, with a rhythmic sound of **languid** water **lap**ping **hypnotic**ally against a beach nearby. As the memory **seep**ed from him into the newchild, he could feel Gabe's sleep ease and deepen. There had been no **stir** at all when Jonas lifted him from the **crib** and placed him gently into the **mold**ed seat.

He knew that he had the remaining hours of night before they would be aware of his escape. So he rode hard, steadily, willing himself not to tire as the minutes and miles passed. There had been no time to receive the memories he and The Giver had counted on, of strength and courage. So he relied on what he had, and hoped it would be enough.

He circled the **outlying** communities, their dwellings

---

* hammock : 해먹. 나무 사이에 달아매는 그물 침대.

dark. **Gradually** the distances between communities widened, with longer stretches of empty road. His legs ached at first; then, as time passed, they became **numb**.

At dawn Gabriel began to stir. They were in an **isolate**d place; fields on either side of the road were dotted with **thicket**s of trees here and there. He saw a stream, and made his way to it across a **rutt**ed, **bumpy meadow**; Gabriel, wide awake now, **giggle**d as the bicycle **jolt**ed him up and down.

Jonas unstrapped Gabe, lifted him from the bike, and watched him **investigate** the grass and **twig**s with delight. Carefully he hid the bicycle in thick bushes.

"Morning meal, Gabe!" He unwrapped some of the food and fed them both. Then he filled the cup he had brought with water from the stream and held it for Gabriel to drink. He drank thirstily himself, and sat by the stream, watching the newchild play.

He was **exhaust**ed. He knew he must sleep, resting his own **muscle**s and preparing himself for more hours on the bicycle. It would not be safe to travel in daylight.

They would be looking for him soon.

He found a place deeply hidden in the trees, took the newchild there, and lay down, holding Gabriel in his arms. Gabe **struggle**d cheerfully as if it were a wrestling game, the kind they had played back in the dwelling, with **tickle**s and laughter.

"Sorry, Gabe," Jonas told him. "I know it's morning, and I know you just woke up. But we have to sleep now."

He **cuddle**d the small body close to him, and rubbed the little back. He **murmure**d to Gabriel soothingly. Then he pressed his hands firmly and transmitted a memory of deep, **contented exhaustion**. Gabriel's head nodded, after a moment, and fell against Jonas's **chest**.

Together the **fugitive**s slept through the first dangerous day.

The most terrifying thing was the planes. By now, days had passed; Jonas no longer knew how many. The journey had become automatic: the sleep by days, hidden in underbrush and trees; the finding of water; the careful division of **scrap**s of food, **augment**ed by what he could find in the fields. And the endless, endless miles on the bicycle by night.

His leg muscles were **taut** now. They ached when he settled himself to sleep. But they were stronger, and he stopped now less often to rest. Sometimes he paused and lifted Gabriel down for a brief bit of exercise, running down the road or through a field together in the dark. But always, when he returned, strapped the uncomplaining toddler into the seat again, and **remount**ed, his legs were ready.

So he had enough strength of his own, and had not needed what The Giver might have provided, had there been time.

But when the planes came, he wished that he could have received the courage.

He knew they were search planes. They flew so low that they woke him with the noise of their engines, and sometimes, looking out and up **fearful**ly from the hiding places, he could almost see the faces of the searchers.

He knew that they could not see color, and that their **flesh**, as well as Gabriel's light golden curls, would be no more than **smear**s of gray against the colorless **foliage**. But he remembered from his science and technology studies at school that the search planes used **heat-seeking device**s which could identify body warmth and would **home in on** two humans **huddle**d in **shrubbery**.

So always, when he heard the **aircraft** sound, he reached to Gabriel and transmitted memories of snow, keeping some for himself. Together they became cold; and when the planes were gone, they would **shiver**, holding each other, until sleep came again.

Sometimes, **urging** the memories into Gabriel, Jonas felt that they were more **shallow**, a little weaker than they had been. It was what he had hoped, and what he and The

Giver had planned: that as he moved away from the community, he would **shed** the memories and leave them behind for the people. But now, when he needed them, when the planes came, he tried hard to **cling** to what he still had, of cold, and to use it for their survival.

Usually the aircraft came by day, when they were hiding. But he was **alert** at night, too, on the road, always listening **intent**ly for the sound of the engines. Even Gabriel listened, and would call out, "Plane! Plane!" sometimes before Jonas had heard the terrifying noise. When the aircraft searchers came, as they did **occasional**ly, during the night as they rode, Jonas sped to the nearest tree or bush, dropped to the ground, and made himself and Gabriel cold. But it was sometimes a **frighten**ingly **close call**.

As he pedaled through the nights, through isolated landscape now, with the communities far behind and no sign of human **habitation** around him or ahead, he was constantly **vigilant**, looking for the next nearest hiding place should the sound of engines come.

But the **frequency** of the planes **diminish**ed. They came less often, and flew, when they did come, less slowly, as if the search had become **haphazard** and no longer hopeful. Finally there was an entire day and night when they did not come at all.

22

Now the landscape was changing. It was a **subtle** change, hard to identify at first. The road was narrower, and **bumpy**, **apparent**ly no longer **tend**ed by road crews. It was harder, suddenly, to balance on the bike, as the front wheel **wobble**d over stones and **ruts**.

One night Jonas fell, when the bike **jolt**ed to a sudden stop against a rock. He grabbed **instinctive**ly for Gabriel; and the newchild, **strap**ped tightly in his seat, was un**in-jure**d, only **frighten**ed when the bike fell to its side. But Jonas's **ankle** was twisted, and his knees were **scrape**d and **raw**, blood **seeping** through his torn **trousers**. Painfully he righted himself and the bike, and **reassure**d Gabe.

Tentatively he began to ride in daylight. He had forgotten the fear of the searchers, who seemed to have diminished into the past. But now there were new fears;

the unfamiliar landscape held hidden, unknown **peril**s.

Trees became more numerous, and the forests beside the road were dark and thick with mystery. They saw streams more frequently now and stopped often to drink. Jonas carefully washed his injured knees, **wincing** as he rubbed at the raw **flesh**. The constant ache of his **swollen** ankle was eased when he **soak**ed it **occasional**ly in the cold water that rushed through roadside **gullies**.

He was newly aware that Gabriel's safety **depend**ed entirely upon his own continued strength.

They saw their first waterfall, and for the first time wildlife.

"Plane! Plane!" Gabriel called, and Jonas turned **swift**ly into the trees, though he had not seen planes in days, and he did not hear an **aircraft** engine now. When he stopped the bicycle in the **shrubbery** and turned to grab Gabe, he saw the small **chubby** arm pointing toward the sky.

Terrified, he looked up, but it was not a plane at all. Though he had never seen one before, he identified it from his fading memories, for The Giver had given them to him often. It was a bird.

Soon there were many birds along the way, **soar**ing overhead, calling. They saw **deer**; and once, beside the road, looking at them curious and unafraid, a small reddish-brown creature with a thick tail, whose name Jonas did not know. He slowed the bike and they stared at one another until the creature turned away and disappeared into the woods.

All of it was new to him. After a life of Sameness and **predictability**, he was **awed** by the surprises that lay beyond each curve of the road. He slowed the bike again and again to look with wonder at wildflowers, to enjoy the **throaty warble** of a new bird nearby, or merely to watch the way wind **shift**ed the leaves in the trees. During his twelve years in the community, he had never felt such simple moments of **exquisite** happiness.

But there were desperate fears building in him now as well. The most **relentless** of his new fears was that they would **starve**. Now that they had left the **cultivate**d fields behind them, it was almost impossible to find food. They finished the **meager** store of potatoes and carrots they had saved from the last **agricultural** area, and now they were always hungry.

Jonas **knelt** by a stream and tried without success to catch a fish with his hands. **Frustrate**d, he threw rocks into the water, knowing even as he did so that it was useless. Finally, in **desperation**, he **fashion**ed a **makeshift** net, **loop**-ing the **strand**s of Gabriel's blanket around a curved stick.

After **countless** tries, the net **yield**ed two **flop**ping

silvery fish. **Methodicall**y Jonas **hack**ed them to pieces with a sharp rock and fed the raw **shred**s to himself and to Gabriel. They ate some berries, and tried without success to catch a bird.

At night, while Gabriel slept beside him, Jonas lay awake, **torture**d by hunger, and remembered his life in the community where meals were delivered to each **dwelling** every day.

He tried to use the **flagg**ing power of his memory to **recreate** meals, and managed brief, **tantalizing fragment**s: **banquet**s with huge roasted meats; birthday parties with thick-**frost**ed cakes; and **lush** fruits picked and eaten, sun-warmed and **dripp**ing, from trees.

But when the memory **glimpse**s **subside**d, he was left with the **gnaw**ing, painful emptiness. Jonas remembered, suddenly and **griml**y, the time in his childhood when he had been **chastise**d for misusing a word. The word had been "starving." You have never been starving, he had been told. You will never be starving.

Now he was. If he had stayed in the community, he would not be. It was as simple as that. Once he had **yearn**ed for choice. Then, when he had had a choice, he had made the wrong one: the choice to leave. And now he was starving.

But if he had stayed . . .

His thoughts continued. If he had stayed, he would have starved in other ways. He would have lived a life hungry for feelings, for color, for love.

And Gabriel? For Gabriel there would have been no life at all. So there had not really been a choice.

It became a **struggle** to ride the bicycle as Jonas weakened from lack of food, and realized at the same time that he was **encounter**ing something he had for a long time yearned to see: hills. His **sprain**ed ankle **throb**bed as he forced the pedal downward in an effort that was almost beyond him.

And the weather was changing. It rained for two days. Jonas had never seen rain, though he had experienced it often in the memories. He had liked those rains, enjoyed the new feeling of it, but this was different. He and Gabriel became cold and wet, and it was hard to get dry, even when sunshine occasionally followed.

Gabriel had not cried during the long frightening journey. Now he did. He cried because he was hungry and cold and terribly weak. Jonas cried, too, for the same reasons, and another reason as well. He wept because he was afraid now that he could not save Gabriel. He no longer cared about himself.

23

Jonas felt more and more certain that the **destination** lay ahead of him, very near now in the night that was approaching. None of his senses confirmed it. He saw nothing ahead except the endless ribbon of road unfolding in twisting narrow curves. He heard no sound ahead.

Yet he felt it: felt that Elsewhere was not far away. But he had little hope left that he would be able to reach it. His hope **diminish**ed further when the sharp, cold air began to **blur** and thicken with **swirl**ing white.

Gabriel, wrapped in his **inadequate blanket**, was **hunch**ed, **shiver**ing, and silent in his little seat. Jonas stopped the bike **wearily**, lifted the child down, and realized with heartbreak how cold and weak Gabe had become.

Standing in the **freezing mound** that was thickening around his **numb** feet, Jonas opened his own **tunic**, held

Gabriel to his **bare chest**, and tied the torn and dirty blanket around them both. Gabriel moved **feebly** against him and **whimper**ed briefly into the silence that surrounded them.

Dimly, from a nearly forgotten perception as blurred as the substance itself, Jonas **recall**ed what the whiteness was.

"It's called snow, Gabe," Jonas whispered. "*Snowflakes.* They fall down from the sky, and they're very beautiful."

There was no response from the child who had once been so curious and alert. Jonas looked down through the **dusk** at the little head against his chest. Gabriel's curly hair was **matted** and **filthy**, and there were tearstains outlined in dirt on his pale cheeks. His eyes were closed. As Jonas watched, a snowflake **drift**ed down and was caught briefly for a moment's **sparkle** in the tiny **flutter**ing **eyelash**es.

Wearily he **remount**ed the bicycle. A **steep** hill **loom**ed ahead. In the best of conditions, the hill would have been a difficult, demanding ride. But now the rapidly deepening snow **obscure**d the narrow road and made the ride impossible. His front wheel moved forward **imperceptibly** as he pushed on the **pedal**s with his numb, **exhaust**ed legs. But the bicycle stopped. It would not move.

He got off and let it drop sideways into the snow. For a moment he thought how easy it would be to drop beside it himself, to let himself and Gabriel slide into the softness of snow, the darkness of night, the warm comfort of sleep.

But he had come this far. He must try to go on.

The memories had fallen behind him now, escaping from his protection to return to the people of his community. Were there any left at all? Could he hold onto a last bit of warmth? Did he still have the strength to Give? Could Gabriel still Receive?

He pressed his hands into Gabriel's back and tried to remember sunshine. For a moment it seemed that nothing came to him, that his power was completely gone. Then it **flickere**d suddenly, and he felt tiny tongues of heat begin to **creep** across and into his frozen feet and legs. He felt his face begin to **glow** and the **tense**, cold skin of his arms and hands relax. For a **fleeting** second he felt that he wanted to keep it for himself, to let himself **bathe** in sunlight, un**burden**ed by anything or anyone else.

But the moment passed and was followed by an **urge**, a need, a **passionate yearn**ing to share the warmth with the one person left for him to love. Aching from the effort, he forced the memory of warmth into the thin, shivering body in his arms.

Gabriel **stir**red. For a moment they both were bathed in warmth and renewed strength as they stood hugging each other in the **blind**ing snow.

Jonas began to walk up the hill.

The memory was **agonizing**ly brief. He had **trudge**d no more than a few yards through the night when it was gone and they were cold again.

But his mind was alert now. Warming himself ever so briefly had shaken away the **lethargy** and **resignation** and **restore**d his will to survive. He began to walk faster on feet that he could no longer feel. But the hill was **treacherous**ly steep; he was **impede**d by the snow and his own lack of strength. He didn't make it very far before he **stumble**d and fell forward.

On his knees, unable to rise, Jonas tried a second time. His consciousness **grasp**ed at a **wisp** of another warm memory, and tried **desperate**ly to hold it there, to **enlarge** it, and pass it into Gabriel. His spirits and strength lifted with the momentary warmth and he stood. Again, Gabriel stirred against him as he began to climb.

But the memory faded, leaving him colder than before.

If only he had had time to receive more warmth from The Giver before he escaped! Maybe there would be more left for him now. But there was no purpose in if-onlys. His entire **concentration** now had to be on moving his feet, warming Gabriel and himself, and going forward.

He climbed, stopped, and warmed them both briefly again, with a tiny **scrap** of memory that seemed certainly to be all he had left.

The top of the hill seemed so far away, and he did not know what lay beyond. But there was nothing left to do but continue. He trudged upward.

As he approached the **summit** of the hill at last, something began to happen. He was not warmer; if anything, he felt more numb and more cold. He was not less exhausted; on the contrary, his steps were **leaden**, and he could **barely** move his freezing, tired legs.

But he began, suddenly, to feel happy. He began to recall happy times. He remembered his parents and his sister. He remembered his friends, Asher and Fiona. He remembered The Giver.

Memories of joy **flood**ed through him suddenly.

He reached the place where the hill **crest**ed and he could feel the ground under his snow-covered feet become level. It would not be uphill anymore.

"We're almost there, Gabriel," he whispered, feeling quite certain without knowing why. "I remember this place, Gabe." And it was true. But it was not a grasping of a thin and burdensome **recollection**; this was different. This was something that he could keep. It was a memory of his own.

He hugged Gabriel and rubbed him **brisk**ly, warming him, to keep him alive. The wind was **bitter**ly cold. The snow swirled, blurring his vision. But somewhere ahead, through the blinding storm, he knew there was warmth and light.

Using his final strength, and a special knowledge that was deep inside him, Jonas found the **sled** that was waiting for them at the top of the hill. Numbly his hands **fumble**d for the rope.

He settled himself on the sled and hugged Gabe close. The hill was steep but the snow was **powdery** and soft, and he knew that this time there would be no ice, no fall, no pain. Inside his freezing body, his heart **surge**d with hope.

They started down.

Jonas felt himself losing consciousness and with his whole being **will**ed himself to stay **upright** atop the sled, **clutch**ing Gabriel, keeping him safe. The runners sliced through the snow and the wind **whip**ped at his face as they sped in a straight line through an **incision** that seemed to lead to the final destination, the place that he had always felt was waiting, the Elsewhere that held their future and their past.

He forced his eyes open as they went downward, downward, sliding, and all at once he could see lights, and he recognized them now. He knew they were shining through the windows of rooms, that they were the red, blue, and yellow lights that **twinkle**d from trees in places where families created and kept memories, where they **celebrate**d love.

Downward, downward, faster and faster. Suddenly he

was aware with certainty and joy that below, ahead, they were waiting for him; and that they were waiting, too, for the baby. For the first time, he heard something that he knew to be music. He heard people singing.

Behind him, across vast distances of space and time, from the place he had left, he thought he heard music too. But perhaps it was only an echo.